GET
A
LIFE

PRINCIPLES FOR
SUCCESS AND ENJOYMENT
IN EVERY AREA OF LIFE

GET
A
LIFE

PRINCIPLES FOR
SUCCESS AND ENJOYMENT
IN EVERY AREA OF LIFE

BRIAN HOUSTON

GET A LIFE (revised business edition)
Copyright © 1999 Brian Houston
educational, motivational

National Library of Australia:
Cataloguing-in-Publication data:

      Houston, Brian.
      Get a life : principles for success and enjoyment in
      every area of life.

      Rev. business ed.
      ISBN 0 9577336 1 5.

      1. Conduct of life. 2. Life skills. 3. Christian life.
      4. Self- help techniques. I. Title.

      158.1

Cover design by CPGD,
Suite 19, 226-271 Pennant Hills Road,
Thornleigh, NSW 2120

Front cover photo image by Asher Gregory.

Printed by Merino Lithographics, Moorooka, Qld.

Published by Brian Houston Ministries
PO Box 1195, Castle Hill, NSW 1765 Australia

"Modo liceat vivere, est spes"

Where there is life there is hope

TERENCE (C.190-159 BC.)

Acknowledgements

Bobbie, Joel, Ben and Laura - I love you.

Thank you to a faithful staff and team. Special mention to those who have been with us since the early days. Your love and loyalty will always be appreciated.

Daryl-Anne Le Roux, Ruth Athanasio and Craig Hingston - thank you for your input.

Bobbie - your help has been invaluable. As always, you have gone above and beyond.

Megan Ivory, Tim Dewhurst and Bec Wood - who else could do what you do?

"The Hills Team", Thank you.

Contents

Endorsements

Jonathan De Jong
Founder, Fantastic Furniture Australia

"This book will change your life. Brian will challenge you to believe in yourself. You will achieve more and go beyond all you dreamed your destiny could be. Read *Get a Life* and it will teach you how to obtain life in all its fullness."

Peter Irvine
Vice Chairman
DDB Needham Worldwide Advertising

"*Get a Life* is a must if you find it challenging to balance every area of your life, progress and actually enjoy the journey. Brian Houston challenges you to not just get by in life - but have a life that is truly successful. Brian shares single-minded and simple challenges that will help you overcome, progress and grab all of life's opportunities. He highlights the 'robbers' of life, such as negativity. Brian applies what he writes and enjoys his life to the full. Get a copy and get a life."

Alan Cadman
Federal Member
Parliamentary Secretary for Work Place and
Small Business

"I have no hesitation in endorsing *Get a Life*. From my experience, one of the greatest dilemmas facing humanity today is their lack of a sense of personal significance.

Brian Houston's presentations and management style are a model for anyone wanting to absorb the theory, practise and ethics of excellence, effectiveness, quality management and team potential. He is an inspiring speaker and uses real life examples which captivate his audience whether they are self employed, looking for work or CEO's of large organisations.

Get a Life is an inspired book which encourages people to go for their highest with confidence. It also warns of the traps which can sabotage potential. I highly recommend this entertaining and persuasive answer to life's problems."

Nabi Saleh
Chairman: Jireh International Pty Ltd
Master Franchise - Gloria Jean's Gourmet
Coffee Australia

"Brian Houston has written a remarkable book, *Get a Life*, in which he outlines how to fulfil your life's potential. Brian shares vital keys straight from his heart and experience. There are some things we need to grow into and other things we need to overcome. The result will be the fulfilment of your dream and vision. He puts into practise, in his own life, all that he has written in this book.

I have no hesitation in recommending this book to all those who want to rise up and excel in all facets of life."

Bill Bassett
Owner and Managing Director of
Interclean Australia Pty Ltd

"Full of great insight and practical wisdom. This is a wonderful book that captures Brian's spirit. It will convince you that there is more life out there to obtain Brian will challenge you to take responsibility in the basic areas of your life. He'll inspire you to look further and run the race of life well."

Don Cooper Williams
Director of Marketing
SAP Australia and New Zealand Pty Ltd

"This book epitomises Brian Houston's philosophy and beliefs. A fresh, radical view that needs to be embraced by all who desire to be leaders or aspire to a life of 'better things'. I recommend it to today's business person who is looking for substance in a sea of motivational mediocrity. Great stuff!"

FORWARD

by Pat Mesiti

C ommon sense is not so common. Wisdom is common sense applied to situations in life. Without wisdom our lives spiral downwards. We become a playground for negativity, doubt, under-achievement, fear and stress. Past hurts and failures can be festering sores in a life that lacks wisdom.

Wisdom gives you perception. It helps you to be motivated. It gives you the ability to not only think creatively, but to go a step further and implement. So where can we obtain wisdom? Look no further than this book written by my friend, Brian Houston. It is full to the brim with practical, ethical and motivational wisdom for getting a life and living it to the fullest.

I have known Brian for over 15 years and am proud to call him my mentor and most importantly, my friend. He lives what he writes and practices what he teaches.

Get A Life is loaded with gems to help you achieve maximum impact for living. It is not recommended - it is required reading for all those who want to be successful and achieve every dream and goal in their life. Be prepared for the challenge and enjoy the journey as you *Get A Life*!

INTRODUCTION

There is a quality that is the possession of every person. It is an inheritance available to all, but claimed by few. This quality is called POTENTIAL. There is a proverb that tells us that "much food [potential] is in the fallow ground of the poor". Just under the surface is an abundant lifestyle, but many people miss it and live frustrated, dissatisfied, underproductive lives.

Potential is "what might be or could be, but does not yet exist."

A young child is seen running around the football or baseball park showing extraordinary flair and skill. With incredible agility and the quick thinking of a veteran he steers his team to victory. Talent scouts mark him as someone who "COULD be anything". Several years later we witness that very same person. He's the overweight storyteller at the bar having one too many drinks, the has-been who COULD HAVE BEEN anything. Through lack of discipline, lack of integrity, lack of determination or wrong choices the young man voted "Most Likely To Succeed" has missed his true potential. In reality this make-believe scenario, is repeated far too many times all around the world.

What is the difference between "should be" and "should have been", or "might be" and "might have been?" It is the fine line between FULFILLED OR FAILED POTENTIAL. It is the fine line between getting a life, or missing it completely.

One day while I was walking through the streets of Sydney with my father, we were almost knocked over by a drunk man who came flying out the front door of a hotel. The smelly, dishevelled man landed on the pavement in front of us, covered in alcohol and vomit. I thought to myself, "This man's life appears to represent a series of wrong choices." His life, like all humanity was full of potential, full of could have been's, but he appeared to be forfeiting his opportunity.

Many people live captive to a victim mentality. A passive, powerless philosophy. This defeated thinking believes you have no control over your future. "Whatever will be, will be. You get what you are given, and that's that."

What a lie! Potential is within every person. Potential to change your world for the better. But in order to have it and utilise it we first have to actively seek it out.

In the hit movie *Forrest Gump*, winner of seven Academy Awards, the central character believed that life was like a box of chocolates: "You never know what you're going to get. Life may hand out challenges and trials and no-one has any influence over the outcome."

Gump's philosophy, which he wisely used to deflect any attempt to put him down, was "Stupid is as stupid does." In other words, you are rewarded according to what you believe about yourself.

If you believe that you're clumsy, you will be. Believe you're unemployable and you won't find a job. Believe you are not worthy of success and you will never achieve anything. And if you believe you are stupid, you will do stupid things.

When I was a young boy at school, a teacher decided to play a game. He lined up the students around the edge of the room and asked each one to spell a word. Any child who failed had to sit down. The well meaning teacher thought this "game" would teach us to spell better, but the game was actually humiliating, and emphasised weakness. The medium is the message.

What you believe IS, sets the tone for your life. That belief then establishes foundations in your life which are vitally important. It is possible for a person to live their entire life on a platform of perception which may be ripping them off. It is imperative that you and I genuinely believe that we have a purpose in life and that we are capable of fulfilling it.

Understanding this then establishes a starting point for realised potential. If you live with a positive foundation and act according to that belief, you will be rewarded.

Helen Keller once said "Life is either a daring adventure, or nothing." How many times has somebody emerged from mediocrity to become great because they had MORE courage, MORE perseverance and MORE faith than the average person? We see this in the sporting arena, music industry, the arts, and it is clearly seen in the business world.

During one of my speaking trips to Queensland, I met a young man who told me his brother lived in my home town of Sydney and captained a football team. I asked which team it was, expecting an answer such as the C Grade Guildford Brawlers, but he replied "The Manly Sea Eagles." Straight away he had my attention. Manly is one of Australia's finest professional rugby league teams.

When I asked who his brother was, I was again impressed. It turned out that he was a famous international footballer who later became a TV commentator and the host of one of the most popular sports shows in the country.

This young man explained that he also had had great potential as a footballer, but a heavy tackle damaged his knees and from that moment his rugby league career was reduced to what could have been.

Rather than take the soft option and retreat to a life of unfulfilled memories and lost potential I'm happy to add that, unlike many people who give up, he changed his focus and is succeeding in other areas. Serious injury could not deter him from achieving great results.

Realising your potential requires that you ignore:

- the limitations and expectations of others.
- the limitations and restraints of your own thinking.
- the limitations of your environment and upbringing.

When you subject yourself to these limitations you

become an underachiever. But when you choose to live according to your potential, you find yourself going above and beyond, far exceeding all limitations.

- ABOVE - discovering the higher way
- BEYOND - going further
- EXCEEDS - easily surpassing

These words describe a life of success, a life that impacts others, and a life of plenty. Now that is not the life of an underachiever.

Napoleon said "Impossible is a word found only in the dictionary of fools." Extraordinary people do extraordinary things. They push past the acceptable levels that many settle for. They push through the barriers that contain and they go over the top in the arena of achievement. They are the kind of people history tends to record.

Much of today's established perception stifles potential. It has people thinking "from behind", from the "bottom of the pile".

This book looks at modern day living in the light of wisdom for the heart. It endeavours to reveal the quality of life available to you. It unlocks the process of claiming that potential, living it to it's maximum and helps you discover fulfilment along the way.

"You only live once, but if you work it right, once is enough." (Joe Lewis)

GET A LIFE! IT'S YOURS FOR THE TAKING!!

COLLIDE WITH LIFE AND DISCOVER YOUR DESTINY

If you think you are beaten, you are;
If you think that you dare not, you don't;
If you'd like to win, but you think you can't,
It's almost certain you won't.

If you think you'll lose, you've lost;
For out in the world you'll find
Success begins with a **fellow's will** -
It's all in the state of mind.

If you think you are outclassed, you are;
You've got to think high to rise;
You've got to be sure of yourself before
You can ever win a prize.

Life's battles don't always go
To the stronger or faster man;
But soon or late **the man who wins
Is the man who thinks he can**."

(Unattributed)

COLLIDE WITH LIFE
AND DISCOVER YOUR DESTINY

You were created with destiny, you are not the result of fate. You are not an accident, and you are not a fluke. No. In fact, at the time of your conception about one million sperm were all fighting for the opportunity to be you. That makes *you* a million to one chance. Destiny is written all over you!

Before Charles Darwin's theory on Evolution ... Destiny. Before Albert Einstein's theory of Relativity... Destiny. Before Shirley Maclaine's theory about total weirdness ... Destiny. Before Christopher Columbus and Captain James Cook ... Destiny. Before Apple Macintosh or IBM ... Destiny. Before Big Macs and Coke ... Destiny. Before you were conceived you had a destiny and now that you are here, you must ask yourself, WHY?

This destiny is not powerless fate. It is pre-determined **purpose**.

All of Creation is held together for a purpose. The stars, the planets, the sea and the great forests sit in place through the cleverness of a mighty Creator. You also, as part of this creation, were designed to live a life that holds together, one that achieves and prospers, grows and moves forward.

HOPE FOR THE HOPELESS

By understanding and cooperating with this Master Plan for your life, you can build a better life than you ever imagined.

You were created to be something and somebody, not nothing and nobody.

When the planet was made it was without form and void - an empty waste land. Then all the intricate beauty that we see around us was created for us - from absolutely nothing. Now there is an answer to the person who feels they are of no value. Outstanding things can emerge from nothing. Nothing can become something, and a seeming nobody can become a significant somebody!

Hope is a wonderful and essential foundation for life, but the absence of hope can cause a life to fall apart. What is it that prevents life from coming unglued? Marriages tend to break down when they're not built on the right foundation. Careers become unstuck when there is no greater purpose holding them together and self-esteem falls apart when people refuse to believe in their real potential and self-worth. Hope is not a flimsy concept. It is one of the pillars upon which this destiny is built.

"Change your thoughts and you can change your world." (Norman Vincent Peale)

SOLOMON'S WISDOM

From 971-931 BC, a famed king named Solomon, ruled in Israel. Known for his remarkable wisdom and insight, today his writings form the foundation for many business and life principles.

Observe these words of Solomon and comprehend this hope:

> "But for him who is joined to all the living there is hope, for a living dog is better than a dead lion!" [1]

Better to be a live dog than a dead lion. While there is life there is hope, and the abundant life available to you, is anything but a dog's life. You were created to live an abundant life, not a redundant life!

You may feel like you're worthless, act like you are worthless, or even believe you are worthless . . but at least you are alive.

FAVOURITISM OR FAVOUR?

Does life favour the beautiful? Do the super-intelligent have an unfair advantage in life? Are multi-talented people the only ones who can look forward to a quality life? Not according to Solomon's wisdom. He also said:

> The race is not to the swift, nor the battle to the strong, nor riches to men of understanding, nor favour to men of skill, but time and chance (opportunity) happen to them all. [2]

He encourages us that winning is not only to the 'swift', that victory is not only for the 'strong', that favour is not just for the 'skilful'. These people do not have exclusive rights to achieving an abundant life.

Solomon said our collision with a future marked with success, is based on time and opportunity. In other words, we all have our time and we all have our chance.

Quality life and destiny is not reserved for a select few. Neither is it automatic, and neither will it produce dissatisfaction, regret or empty memories.

Many so-called "beautiful people" and celebrities live dissatisfied because they are ruled by what they don't like about themselves or don't have. Business people live in regret recalling the boom times before the big recession. Retired sportsmen may fill their days reliving former glories, trapped within a time warp of the good ol' days. We all need to understand that despite the state of our past (and even our present), a great future awaits us all.

We all exist for a unique purpose. We each have an individual purpose - a calling, a destiny. This Life-Destiny involves hard work, persistence, resilience, accomplishment and fulfilment, and according to Solomon's wisdom time and opportunity deliver it into our experience.

Nelson Mandela emerged from twenty seven years in prison to become the leader of his nation. It was his, and his people's time. An opportunity that has changed the face of South Africa, and marked Nelson Mandela as a man of destiny.

Sir Winston Churchill stated "I felt as if I were walking with destiny, and that all my past life had been but a preparation for this hour and this trial."

Neil Armstrong became the first man to set foot on the moon's surface. He made that historically famous statement: "One small step for man, one giant leap for mankind." It was his and his nation's time.

Victor Hugo, author of *Les Miserables* and many other great literary works during the 19th century, is quoted as saying "There is one thing stronger than all the armies in the world, and that is an idea whose time has come."

Les Miserables was attributed as "a religious work", with the 'air of having been written by God'. Victor recognised his time and opportunity and was immortalised for it.

You also have your own time and chance here on earth.

Pop art painter and sculptor Andy Warhol said "every man has his 15 minutes of fame". The life you can enjoy is designed to be so much more than 15 minutes in a spotlight. It is designed to be a full and long life that winds upward and moves forward. A life designed to be rewarding and fulfilling, impacting and valuable.

What greater tragedy is there, than our inclination to live below our potential? Are we changing our surroundings or are we being squashed by them? Are we conforming, when we should be transforming?

Is it possible for each one of us to break free, from whatever may contain us and embrace this time and opportunity? From my experience in dealing and working with multiplied hundreds of people, I believe it is possible. However, it is a matter of choice.

DON'T LET THE PAST SABOTAGE YOUR FUTURE

Solomon goes on to say:

> For man also does not know his time; like fish taken in a cruel net, like birds caught in a snare. [4]

Many people never collide with this life and this Destiny, because they spend all of their energy trying to get free. Rather than channel their energy on the future and potential new horizons, they are ruled or consumed with past hurts, problems or failings. All their energy is spent focusing on these things.

This wise proverb says that the man or woman who misses this truth is like 'the fish in a cruel net or the bird in a snare'. These creatures don't die immediately, but use up every ounce of energy trying to obtain freedom. The bird flaps itself to exhaustion. The fish fights pathetically until it has nothing left.

You will never collide with your destiny if you are trapped in a continuous cycle of thought patterns, lifestyle choices and negative habits dictated by your background.

You do not have to be a victim of your past.

A failed relationship need not devastate your trust forever. An abused childhood should not mean you have to live a dysfunctional life. And a crippled past need not pollute your personality.

If you are devoting all of your emotional resources to "breaking free" from the attitudes and circumstances of past experiences, you have neither the time nor the energy to pursue your predetermined purpose.

BREAK FREE TO LIVE FREE

Can you imagine the wasted potential in the poverty stricken, undeveloped nations of the world? Because potential remains uncultivated, there are millions of people across these continents who may never collide with their destinies. Poverty, corruption and government dictatorships are amongst the things that hold them back. Potential business leaders, concert pianists, inventors, surgeons and engineers cannot realise their true value.

In the same way, people in prosperous developed nations who flap around, unable to break free from what entangles them emotionally, become the "living poor", because of their impoverished state of thinking.

Life is brief and precious and should not be consumed with trying to break free. To GET A LIFE one must first get free! To GET A LIFE one needs to discover the freedom already available to us. To GET A LIFE one needs to discover "a higher purpose".

Psychology, counselling or self-help courses all have certain validity, but the day comes when **you** have to take hold of your life, and with wisdom and courage, apply the principles and disciplines which will enable you to live free of entanglement. You will then begin to collide with a powerful life.

"You alone are responsible for achieving a satisfying life." (*Verome Puchkoff - Chairman & CEO of A.A.I.*)

DESTINY: IT'S GOT YOUR NAME ON IT

A study into the root meaning of the words time and chance, paints these images:

- Imagine destiny is a piece of land with your name inscribed on the title deed. That property is your inheritance. You own it, but you have to lay claim to it before you can possess it. If you don't, the deed stays filed away in the drawer. In your pursuit of that land, there will be discouragements, distractions and the temptation to give up. But it's your time and chance - pursue it. The land may represent many things. Perhaps a business opportunity or an unfulfilled goal. Don't miss your time or chance - collide and claim it.

- Imagine a collision with an enemy which is so violent and bloody that there can only be one winner who eventually falls on his foe victorious.

- You can collide with enemies in your life with such power that they collapse under the weight of your vision. Bad attitude, hurt, mistrust, physical or mental abuse will all fall victim to your faith and hope in your future.

- Imagine a collision so passionate and dramatic that it changes the course of everything forever.

Again, this word study makes it clear that life's race is not only for the strong, the intellectual, the wealthy, the good looking, or those possessing extraordinary skills. These are not the determining qualities.

Whilst you have breath, you have life. Whilst you have life, fulfilled destiny awaits you. What we are about to discover are valuable keys to unlocking this destiny.

TAKE ACTION

1. **Believe** that you are on earth for a higher purpose.

2. **Determine** to discover and collide with your Destiny.

3. **Co-operate** with the higher purpose for your life

4. **Assess** whether your energy is absorbed by old issues or focused on future possibilities.

5. **Decide** what attitudes should be addressed in order to effect change.

CHAPTER TWO

NEGATIVITY IS AN ENEMY TO LIFE

"In the face of unexpected and seemingly hopeless circumstances you have to hold on to your dream."

Negativity Reflects Inner Defeat

Negativity Always Justifies Itself

Negativity Chooses Your Friends

NEGATIVITY IS AN ENEMY TO LIFE

If a collision with a future filled with prosperity, hope, abundance, achievement is a right belonging to us all, why is it that many never achieve it? What is it that keeps "ordinary people" from becoming extraordinary people?

One of the greatest enemies to such achievement is NEGATIVITY.

- Negativity is the verbalisation of inner defeat.

- Negativity reflects a person's outlook on life and,

- Negativity is coloured by their inner self.

A negative outlook, coupled with negative speech can be amongst the most limiting and polluting factors in the lives of multitudes. A great percentage of such people are unaware of the impact this negativity is having on them. It can literally sabotage their destiny and rob them of a fulfilling abundant life.

Are you ruled by what "might" happen or what you "think" you can't afford? Do you see the container "half empty" or "half full"? Human nature, for example is quick to notice the 10% unemployment rate, but rarely focuses on the 90% who are employed.

When a business person, minister or politician fails morally or financially, the public sit up and take notice. Human nature will focus on the failure, but of course for every leader who falls, there are thousands of faithful men and women who over a lifetime, diligently live by good ethics.

Have you ever complimented somebody on a positive aspect of their personality or appearance and they immediately focus on the things you didn't mention. Why? Negativity. Once after a speaking engagement someone said to me "That's the best I've ever heard you speak." I caught myself wondering what was wrong with the other times, rather than simply appreciating the encouragement.

In your day-to-day life do you ever listen to yourself speak? Do you notice the anxiety you express or the hopelessness you confess? This shows up in even the simplest comments. It's like the man who is greeted at home in the evening by his wife with a big kiss. She tells him she saw a beautiful dress in the store. Because he loves her, he encourages her to go back and buy it, but she may reply:

"The store will probably be closed" or

"The dress was so nice it has probably gone" or

"Do you really think we can afford it?"

His wife dare not hope for the best, so she prepares herself for the worst. It's human nature, but it can be changed.

Negativity has the power to trap you. It will hold you down well below your potential, and cause you to miss out on the exciting plan for your life. As is often quoted "I have never seen a monument erected to a pessimist!"

It is not so much an issue of who is negative or positive. It is more a matter of understanding, that to lay hold of the future that is rightfully yours, and to collide with your destiny, overcoming negativity must be a daily decision.

Why is negativity so powerful? Why is it so dangerous? Let's take a look at this over the next two chapters. There are eight reasons why you need to defeat it NOW, in order to achieve your potential.

NEGATIVITY REFLECTS INNER DEFEAT

For out of the abundance of the **heart** the mouth speaks.

You can easily tell the content of a person's heart by listening to the words they speak. The abundance is located in their speech. Negativity is a sure sign of inner defeat.

I once received a tragic letter from a woman who was outlining the sad details of her marriage breakup. The more I read, the more obvious it became that she blamed the actions of many other people. Perhaps her negative feelings toward her former husband were understandable, but it went beyond that.

In her letter, she went on to recount the many and varied actions of particular people, up to 20 years prior.

For example, she attacked not only her former husband but his employer, her employer, her children's school teachers, her church and so on. She went on to explain how she sensed undue pressure from people and how she believed she could never measure up. She felt neither understood nor cared about.

As I read on I began to realise that not all of the blame belonged to others. A large part of her problem was the condition of her own soul. She was totally consumed with self pity and victimisation, and showed no sign of accountability in terms of her own mistakes, motives and attitudes. Her defeated outlook was controlling her entire life.

Negativity always reflects inner defeat. It often lashes out at circumstances, people, the environment or the government. It may focus on a father, mother, leader, boss or spouse. A business may often be a target for negativity, but I believe that IN EVERY CIRCUMSTANCE negativity is not about any of these things. It is about THE INDIVIDUAL.

NEGATIVITY ALWAYS JUSTIFIES ITSELF

We can generally justify the way we think and act. There are usually good reasons for us to feel hurt or perhaps victimised. I can justify my attitudes and reactions, but *justifying won't change anything*. It simply gives me a reason to accept mediocrity or failure .

I recall an occasion when I sat on a committee of prominent Australian leaders and listened with interest to the tone of one of their conversations. One leader spoke continually about his peers in disparaging terms. He used words like "hype" and displayed unmistakable cynicism in his tone. As I listened I couldn't help but think about the course his own life had taken over the past few years. The organisation he led, though a good one, had clearly settled down and had lost the razor sharp edge it enjoyed a decade ago. Could all of his cynicism and sarcasm be negativity, justifying a lack of progress in his own life and work?

Another man preceded his own comments by saying, "I know people are going to call me negative, but people always call you negative when they disagree with you."

Wrong. People call you negative because you are negative.

When an individual becomes negative about the success of others, they are often justifying the lack of progress in their own life. When fingers are pointed at a business person who has worked hard and yet has still gone broke, those cynics are more often than not, justifying their own negativity about hard work. When people are struggling with the concept of winning and achieving, they will find a reason to criticise. They look for examples to justify their stance but then, negativity always tries to justify itself.

Lift Your Expectation Level

I refuse to bring my expectations down to the level of my experience. I am committed to lifting my experience UP to the level of my expectation.

Excuses and reason will combine to pull people, who were once on the "cutting edge", back to a position of stagnant mediocrity.

There was a young man on my staff whose uncle was a leader in a large religious organisation that was declining in numbers because of a stagnant attitude. This old minister maligned his nephew's zest for life, whilst vigorously justifying his own refusal to change, and his commitment to tradition. He repeatedly insisted his nephew's ambition and idealism would change when he had more experience of life.

Negativity attempts to justify its stance by quoting experience. Religion sometimes justifies itself through tradition and experience. However we must stand firm in our determination to succeed, because the moment we begin to justify ourselves we'll cut off opportunities to change and grow.

I once conducted a funeral for a lovely family whose mother had died of breast cancer. During the service I looked over at her teenage children and was moved to see them mourning their mother. When speaking to one of the daughters later, she displayed total determination to succeed in life "for her mum's sake."

In the face of unexpected and seemingly hopeless circumstances you have to hold on to your dream. Experience should not alter your expectation and you should never adjust downward to the level of life's difficulties.

Negative people draw on negative experiences and build their beliefs and opinions around them. Then they justify their position because of what happened to them. Positive people are committed to changing themselves to line up with their potential.

NEGATIVITY CHOOSES YOUR FRIENDS

There is a proverb which says:

He who walks with wise men will be wise, but the **companion of fools** will be destroyed. [6]

In a nutshell, negativity is foolishness. It is foolishness because it creates a confession contrary to success. Negativity is also foolishness because it limits people and colours their outlook. And it is foolishness because it is contagious and spreads very quickly. The companion of fools will be destroyed. It is not fate which destroys them but their foolishness - the foolishness of being negative.

You must be very careful who you spend your time with. Who do you allow to give you advice?

- Are these people moving onward and upward?

- Are they colliding with their destinies and pursuing their dreams?

- Are their words inspiring you to become the person you were intended to be, or are they deflating and distracting you?

- Are they wallowing in negativity, self-pity and mediocrity, going nowhere fast?

Whatever direction your friends are heading in, will have a major influence on your future ... if you allow it.

Positive People Irritate Negative People

A person suffering from negativity gets very annoyed with positive people. A positive confession poses a threat to their negativity. They think such people "surface" or "superficial", living in a shallow world of make-believe with no depth. They will say such things as, "I'm not being negative, I'm being real", or "Why can't he just be real? Why can't he talk about how he really feels and stop putting on this act? He's so out of touch with reality!"

Negative thinkers prefer the company of those who "understand" them and they certainly don't want to be around anyone who confronts them, or whose bright outlook on life challenges their pessimistic way of thinking. As a result, a negative person is unlikely to have lasting friendships with positive people.

Without doubt, negativity chooses your friends.

Like Attracts Like

I never cease to be amazed at the ability of negative people to find each other in a crowd. In the offices of a large company, defeated people drift together and share their criticisms with each other. Whether it's in a sports club or school classroom the same thing happens.

Most business leaders have experienced supposedly well-meaning members of their organisation offering advice like, "Everybody is saying the job is too hard" or "Everybody is saying the company isn't caring enough." If you ask who is "Everybody," the typical response is, "I don't feel at liberty to say."

Ask them exactly how many people are making these comments and generally "Everybody" is two or three. A big "Everybody" could be four! To a negative person those four dissenting voices sound like an overwhelming mass of unanimous support because that's all they are tuned in to.

Like attracts like. Negative thinkers surround themselves with other like thinkers. It makes them feel better about themselves. But even negative friends tire of negativity after a while, and leave their fellow critics isolated.

> A man who isolates himself seeks his own desire; he rages against all wise judgement. [7]

This is how it works: a negative person is so consumed by his own desire or self-centred needs, that he cuts himself off and becomes an island. According to the preceding proverb he rages against all wise judgement. In other words he's not thinking straight. He's behaving like an idiot!

If you are in a situation where you hear a lot of negativity, ask yourself why. Why are doubters, sceptics and critics telling you how they feel? Why do they feel comfortable about dumping their negatives on you? Positive people don't tend to hear "verbal garbage" because they are too much of a threat. They are too optimistic, too loyal, too confronting.

Me, Myself And I

You always know when you have spent time with a negative person because they are so emotionally draining. Most of their attention is focused on themselves. They have little time or concern for others' needs. Negative thinkers want people to understand them - to feel their pain, cry with them, sympathise with them. Of course, empathy is a part of true friendship but like all communication it needs to be a two-way street. If you don't deposit into a relationship, you get the same result as if you didn't make a deposit into your bank account. There is nothing to withdraw. When a negative person builds around "Me", "My problems" and "My needs", their relationships are put into over-draft and eventually bankrupted.

Self-indulgence is an enemy to building the kinds of friendships around you which will enhance a quality life. Solomon wrote, that a faithful friend is prepared to speak the truth to you even though it may risk hurting you.

Faithful are the wounds of a friend.[8]

It takes a friend to care enough to confront key issues in your life and do it in a loving way. Someone who didn't care wouldn't bother. A negative person is more likely to talk about you behind your back.

Negative people don't see instruction as encouragement or an opportunity to change. They believe they are being "dumped on" again.

Can't you just hear them? "All my life people have put me down and now you're doing it too. I thought you were going to be different."

Negative attitudes, perceptions and thoughts are "excess baggage" on our journey through life. Not only are they bulky and heavy, slowing down progress, but they are totally unnecessary.

A person determined to overcome negativity and fulfil their destiny cannot afford to be held back by leadweight relationships.

We should love people and want to help them, but it is essential that leadweight relationships are not given the opportunity to ensnare and sink us. It's always sad in life when you see good people lose their focus because their thinking was infiltrated by the destructive perceptions of others.

If you are fighting any negativity and want to over-come it, you must choose your friends carefully. Associate with those whose outlook and conversation encourage and motivate you to attempt greater things.

TAKE ACTION

1. **Decide** that you will not allow negativity to be a limiting factor in your life.

2. **Remember** to lift your experience to the level of your expectation.

3. **Make** overcoming negativity a daily decision.

4. **Determine** you are not going to be ruled by the "What if's".

5. **Commit** yourself to positive speech (and thoughts).

6. **Refuse** to justify your negativity - change it.

7. **Choose** your friends carefully. You'll never soar with eagles while you are scratching with turkeys.

CHAPTER THREE

NEGATIVITY WILL DISTORT YOUR LIFE

"If we see the light at the end of the tunnel
It's the light of the oncoming train."

(Robert Lowell)

"None so blind as those who will not see."

Negativity Magnifies And Distorts The Truth.

Negativity Makes Harsh Judgements and Unfair Statements.

Negativity Negates The Power Of Life.

Negativity Affects The Generations.

Negativity Limits The Present and Sabotages The Future.

NEGATIVITY WILL DISTORT YOUR LIFE

We have already seen how negativity affects people. It causes them to justify destructive thinking, it impacts their friendships, it allows them to identify with like-minded "feel sorry for yourself" attitudes. Such associations have the power to distract us from our destiny.

Another reason why the fight against negativity in your life must begin today, is that it has the capacity to UNBALANCE many aspects of life.

NEGATIVITY MAGNIFIES AND DISTORTS THE TRUTH

Anxiety in the heart of man causes depression, but a **good word** makes it glad. [9]

Many of Solomon's proverbs are very specific about this subject, particularly in the areas of stress, fear and anxiety. Anxiety is built on what MIGHT happen. It affects every area of your life, and thrives on "What ifs ...?"

- "What if I get sick?"

- "What if I lose my job?"

- "What if my children have an accident?"

Be Anxious for Nothing

Anxiety and fear reveal a lack of confidence and hope. An anxious or depressed person cannot see straight. Their perspective on life is blown out of all proportion. Small things seem huge, molehills turn into unbeatable mountains.

Note the progression in the previous proverb. If negativity, rather than "good words", are in your heart, it will lead to anxiety, and anxiety has the capacity to decline into depression. Giving in to defeated thoughts, allowing them to linger in your mind and occupy your soul, will eventually plunge you into a bottomless pit of depression and fear.

Negativity will bind and cripple you, preventing any hope of progress in your life. In fact, negativity makes the light at the end of the tunnel seem like an on-coming train!

I knew of one man who, in the midst of his depression, was crying because of the possibility that his car might not start in the morning, despite the fact that there was nothing wrong with it. Depression had built problems into his mind that didn't exist. Even though the problem was imagined, it was overtaking his life.

This man was also gripped with a fear that he was

about to die. He was being held captive by his negative thought-life and his depression. His perspective on life was totally askew. He was physically healthy and yet his soul was consumed with negative thoughts and depression.

The Power of Perception

You should never underestimate the power of what you believe, even if it is only a perception. When you believe something, that belief becomes as powerful as if it were the truth. Both truth and perception have equal potential to powerfully influence reality.

For example, if a "rumour" spread that a certain bank had financial problems, it is possible that lines of panic-stricken customers would flood in and withdraw their life savings. Despite being an unfounded rumour, it would have a devastating impact, no less damaging than if it was the truth. The instant drain of funds caused by PERCEPTION could lead to the REALITY of a potentially destroyed bank.

Negativity without doubt, affects your perception.

Remember, your outlook depends on what you are looking out from!

If you are looking at the world from a heart full of cynicism and bitterness, your perspective of the truth more than likely, will become magnified and distorted in a destructive way.

It's amazing that people with equal capacity to see and hear, can witness situations or conversations and interpret them so differently. I remember an occasion when I was asked to mediate between two men who had been partners in a business endeavour. They were disputing the amount of money each was owed.

I was perplexed as I listened to them recount dramatically differing facts. I don't believe either was lying and it seemed they both fully believed "their own story". How could they differ so much?

Perception!

Peoples' perceptions and conclusions about life are coloured by their outlook. A depressed or defeated person may struggle to accept their potential, and even if they can get their head around the concept of success, they often can't get it into their soul. This means their thinking (and therefore their potential) is limited by a deep-seated belief that won't allow them to absorb this hope.

Something that brings great encouragement and is obvious to the majority, can be interpreted totally different by a person with a negative mindset.

Recently I watched a television show where people were being introduced to a studio audience before being "made over" and given a new look.

One man looked fearsome when first introduced to the crowd. He was a giant, with so much hair and an "out of control" beard, that you literally couldn't see his face. His wife likened him to a teddy bear, but appearances did not give that impression.

A teenage girl appeared to have gone to great lengths to look "less than attractive" and the others certainly looked like they too could do with the make over.

The results were stunning. The "hairy" giant emerged sharp and handsome, and the teenage girl was incredibly pretty. Everyone agreed with the dramatic improvement in their appearance, but they all responded the same way: "It looks okay, but it's just not me."

I believe their response was about the way they saw themselves. They had a certain image of themselves and dressed accordingly.

My very good friend Pat Mesiti says "someone who begins with a wrong perception, built on wrong assumptions, can come to all the wrong conclusions, for all the right reasons"!

So true. Here's an example.

Imagine that one day as you are walking down the street, you spy a familiar face in the crowd. It's an old friend you haven't seen for ages. You eagerly approach them but they don't even acknowledge you and appear to look right through you as they walk on by. If negativity rules your soul you might feel as though they ignored you on purpose. A scenario starts to take shape in your heart.

It convinces you that there was an underlying reason for the friend to walk straight past - "They think they're too good for me. They're too busy to stop and say hello. They never did like me."

From that moment your thinking towards that person has become coloured and polluted by this one experience. The *truth* is that the long lost friend was simply in a hurry and didn't see you, but your relationship with them is now clouded by your perceptions.

Our ability to magnify and distort the truth must be recognised before we can effect change.

NEGATIVITY MAKES HARSH JUDGEMENTS AND UNFAIR STATEMENTS

History records how on one particular morning the great Hebrew King, David, was so overwhelmed with happiness and joy that in the presence of a large crowd he began to dance.

According to the Hebrew translation of the word "dance", David was whirling around wildly. He was captivated with excitement and was unrestrained by the opinions of those around him.

King David's wife, Michal, was furious. She felt humiliated. When the King arrived home she got stuck into him. I suppose Michal thought it was beneath their station in life to behave in such a manner. Embarrassment fuelled her caustic and sarcastic retort. "How inglorious was the King of Israel today." She was embarrassed and was accusing the King of making a fool of himself.

Was David's dancing the real issue? Or was it the negative condition of Michal's heart that prompted her to make such harsh judgements?

My family and I live in a nice leafy suburb in Sydney. We love the area for its beauty and we feel it's a great environment for raising our children. It's also the centre for our life and work.

This suburb also has many attractive homes. From time to time, a long-term and much loved friend of ours comes to visit but will make disparaging judgements about the houses near us.

We could easily be offended, but instead we choose to smile, knowing that the real issue is not aesthetics, but has much more to do with the defeat in our friend's soul.

I love the picture painted in the famous analogy of the log and speck; it describes a judgemental person, with a great tree protruding from their eye.

And why do you look at the **speck** in your brother's eye, but do not consider the **plank** in your own eye?[10]

Can you imagine the havoc this person would cause? Everywhere they turned people would have to duck to miss getting thumped by the plank! Isn't it just like that with judgemental people? They are very "speck" conscious.

In a restaurant such people will make judgements about people sitting at other tables: what they're wearing; how they're sitting; the way they're eating; how much they are eating, and so on. Don't sit down and watch TV with them. It's even worse! The program is constantly interrupted with complaints about the acting, the number of ads or the newsreader's clothes.

These "speck" conscious people will criticise anything from the behaviour of today's young people, to the double crease in someone's trousers.

Everywhere they turn, they make harsh, negative judgements and, with their big "telegraph poles" protruding from their eyes, everyone around them has to duck or risk being whacked.

Negativity causes supposedly logical, level- headed people to make rash statements about complete strangers. They form opinions about people they know nothing about.

The Royal Family, presidents, prime ministers and public figures are judged and criticised from a distance. At times broad-sweeping, negative assumptions may even be made about people who are closer to you. Of course, these presumptive statements are the product of a typically negative outlook.

Angry Anderson is a well known rock musician in Australia who spends a lot of his time helping kids. He's short, stocky, heavily tattooed and shaves his head. Without doubt, there are those who would have made assumptions about him based solely on his appearance. I wonder if these same people know of Angry's public concern and compassion for the underprivileged.

I saw him interviewed on a current affair program where he was organising a playground for a school for deaf and blind children. I have a nephew who attended that school and so it was with much interest that I watched as Angry coordinated the project. It included landscaped gardens, pergolas, play areas and even a monorail. However, it all had to be completed in fifty hours.

As the cameras followed Angry contacting various construction companies and seeking their help, I noticed that one concrete supplier donated many tonnes of concrete. I imagined the General Manager of that concrete company driving home in his nice car, possibly a Mercedes Benz or BMW. A negative person passing him in the street might say "That fat cat drives around in such an expensive car and ignores the needy. What would he know about the poor?"

Of course, such a judgement would be terribly unfair, as that "fat cat" had just given away tens of thousands of dollars worth of concrete. Many wealthy people are very supportive of community organisations and they enjoy helping the needy.

The unsubstantiated criticism of a hard living rock

star turned ambassador, and of a successful, very generous businessman are both incorrect perceptions, yet are typical of negativity which makes unfair statements and sweeping judgements.

Back to the playground. Businesses donated materials and tradesmen volunteered their time free of charge. They were faced with numerous challenges including torrential rain, yet miraculously the project was finished on time. I loved seeing the joy it brought to those kids.

NEGATIVITY NEGATES THE POWER OF MOTIVATION

The English word "power" has a number of origins. One of them is a Greek word, "dunamis". From this same root word we have words like dynamite, dynamo and dynamic.

Motivation can be defined as an explosive power and impelling movement. Successful people have this dynamic power operating in them. It enables them to live motivated and progressive lives. They are empowered to get up when they are knocked down and to overcome every setback.

"He's a **dynamo**. He just keeps going."

"She's **dynamic**. She is so motivated."

It is the power of motivation that will keep you energised. It gives you reason to get out of bed in the morning and when necessary, work into the small hours of the night.

And "dunamis" power's greatest enemy? Negativity! Nothing will negate motivation quicker than negativity. To negate means to nullify and neutralise.

Negativity causes people to live powerless, de-motivated lives. If you don't believe you could ever own your own home, it's unlikely you will have the motivation to pursue one.

Negativity does nothing to change your circumstance. It accepts and excuses. It breeds a hopelessness that leads some to defeated behaviour such as alcoholism, overeating or substance abuse.

It is difficult to understand the thinking behind vandalism. There seems to be nothing to gain by destroying someone else's property. Some people are so gripped by the de-motivating powerlessness of negativity, that they become destructive and anti-social.

For some, life has become so negative and futile, that picking up the remote control for the television has become an effort. Meanwhile, the lawns are growing out of control and the garden is a bed of weeds. The car is unwashed, unregistered and uninsured. The dog is flea ridden and the number of little jobs around the house that are not yet done, are mounting daily... All of this serves only one purpose - it enlarges the sense of negativity, which in turn amplifies the sense of powerlessness and intensifies de-motivation. It is a crippling cycle.

There is a psychological condition known as 'catatonic schizophrenia' where sufferers literally freeze on the spot, afraid that if they move they will be punished. Their negative and defeated thought processes paralyse them.

Hopefully, things are not that drastic for you but the power of negativity needs to be broken in order to release the power of motivation in your life.

NEGATIVITY AFFECTS THE GENERATIONS

Train up a child in the way he should go ... when he is old he will not depart from it.

- "I'll never be like my parents" is a common teen-age statement.

- A girl is victimised by her nagging mother and says "I'll never be like that."

- A teary-eyed boy watches his alcoholic father stagger through the house and is determined never to be a drinker.

- A stressed parent screams at the children. The kids retort "We'll never speak to our children like that."

- Children who suffer the pain of divorce commit themselves to never seeing it happen in their own lives.

Yet incredibly, when a large percentage of these young people reach adulthood, they reproduce the very things they despised in their parents. Why is that?

Many children are unable to depart from the way they are brought up. They have been trained in a certain way and are unable to leave it. They become prisoners to the very things they loathe and it takes a miracle or a determined transformation of their thinking, to break free.

A legacy of negative input is NOT what children need. Our example as parents, moulds the personalities of our children in their formative years. Their view of the world is largely shaped by what we do and say.

A stronghold is a fortified enclosure, and when used in reference to the mind, a stronghold is a mindset or way of thinking which captivates and controls that person.

It is imperative that as parents, we don't build negative strongholds into our children's thinking - strongholds which may rule and limit them in their adult life. Strongholds which could easily affect the quality of life of even their own offspring.

Many sad tales are told of people who have never broken the shackles of negativity which were embedded into their lives from childhood.

The story is told of a father who had twin sons. One son was an optimist, the other a pessimist. On the twins' birthday, while the boys were at school, the father loaded the pessimist's room with every imaginable toy and game. The optimist's room he loaded with horse manure.

That night the father passed by the pessimist's room and found him sitting amongst his new gifts crying bitterly. "Why are you crying?" the father asked. "Because my friends will be jealous, and I'll have to read the instructions, and I'll constantly need batteries, and my toys will get broken," answered the pessimist. Passing the optimist's room, the father found him dancing for joy in the pile of manure. "What are you so happy about?" asked the father. The optimist replied, "There's got to be a pony in here somewhere!"

If you can change your outlook, you will also change the inheritance and the course of future generations.

NEGATIVITY LIMITS THE PRESENT AND SABOTAGES THE FUTURE

Negativity pulls things down to their lowest common denominator.

It pulls down potential ladened expectation with "I can't do that," "I could never try this," "I can't live like that" or "I could never look like that!" These are catchcries of an inwardly defeated person.

"I'm just . . ." becomes a regular confession.

- "I'm just an average student."

- "I'm just a poor person, I'll never live in a better house or drive a new car."

- "I'm just so normal, there's no way I could achieve that!"

This is why negativity is such a limiting factor in living the higher way of life available to you. Limited, powerless thinking reduces you to your expectation level, or even lower.

As a small boy I stood on top of the high dive springboard, wanting to dive into the pool that seemed a mile below (it was actually only five metres). Day after day I would stand on the edge too afraid to dive. Lines of people would wait impatiently behind me shouting at me to hurry up, but every time I retreated to firm ground and safety. One day my brother, who was tired of waiting, sneaked up behind me and pushed me in. Surprise, surprise! It was a painless experience. Double pike with reverse twist. 9.5, 9.4, 9.5, 9.6, 9.9!

From that moment onward, diving from the five-metre board was no longer an issue. As long as I had believed I couldn't do it, my negativity succeeded in sabotaging my potential.

It's a simple story, but it illustrates the many areas in our lives where negativity can dominate. There are so many good people whose lives are lived like that. So much potential and so much enjoyment is lost by the perceived limitations of their thinking. The quality of their life falls far short of their true potential.

Decide to challenge negativity in your life and confront it face-to-face. You will gain great satisfaction as you begin to increase the quality of your life and become more of the person you were created to be.

TAKE ACTION

1. **Mentally give up** your concerns and worries.

2. **Speak** positive words of hope and negate anxiety.

3. **Build** your perceptions on TRUTH and not on what MIGHT happen.

4. **Look** for good in everyone and avoid sweeping statements and generalisations.

5. Be **empowered** by a positive outlook.

6. **Create** a positive legacy for the next generation from which they will never waver.

7. **Replace** "I can't" in your vocabulary with "I can".

CHAPTER FOUR

YOUR OUTLOOK IS YOUR VIEW OF LIFE

"The greatest revolution of our generation is the discovery that human beings, by **changing the inner attitudes of their minds**, can change the outer aspects of their lives."

WILLIAM JAMES

Revolutionise Your Soul

Hearing Verses Doing and
Achieving?

Wisdom Is Applied Knowledge

Your Soul Will Shrink It

You Decide

A Prosperous Soul

YOUR OUTLOOK IS
YOUR VIEW OF LIFE

You don't have to live your life as a prisoner to negativity. You can make a daily decision to overcome a negative outlook and transform the way you think.

So, the million dollar question is HOW?

Negativity is simply a reflection of a defeated soul. Transformation must begin in your soul, which is the seat of your thinking, your emotions and your will. Your soul is the real you. It is who you are on the inside, and unless change first occurs in your soul, you will never effect true and lasting change in your external habits and behaviour.

Ask yourself the question - From childhood to becoming an adult, what has really changed in my life? Obviously, there will be physical changes, but just how deep do the changes go?

Does negativity continue to raise its ugly head? Do you fight anxiety? Do you still have bouts of anger or depression? Are you in control of your emotions or are they controlling you?

Your outlook is determined by what you are LOOKING OUT FROM. Change begins with the inner you. The quality of your life will either be restricted by a defeated soul or enlarged by a victorious, positive one.

Far too many people have an EXTERNAL concept regarding change. I remember hearing a rhyme when I was young: "I don't smoke, I don't drink, I don't chew, and I don't go out with girls that do."

It amazes me that some people may appear "model citizens" yet the real change in their lives is about as superficial as this rhyme. They dress right, look right, carry themselves right, mix with all the right people and are seen in all the right places. But has their penchant for gossip stopped? Has their harshness towards their spouse or children ended? Does ceaseless nagging and criticism still rule their present?

You may have perfected a very controlled public image, but if you are still living on an emotional roller coaster, just how controlled are you really? If you are continually bombarded with negative thoughts about yourself and life, how genuine is that image which you present to others?

The sad truth is that there are good people who have all the external evidence of success, but their emotions are in turmoil and their thinking is defeated. No wonder they haven't yet collided with their destiny. Change must begin internally.

REVOLUTIONISE YOUR SOUL

You will never change by merely trying to alter the outward habits or circumstances around you.

A house may have a beautiful facade and an immaculately manicured garden, but such things are not the indicators of the quality of life for those living within its walls. If the occupants are filled with sadness and unhappiness, the exterior is merely a front or facade. This is also how it is with our lives. The issues happening internally are the things that locate who we really are.

When a horticulturalist engrafts two trees together they become one. In a similar way a more positive attitude can be engrafted into the arena of our soul. Negative behaviour will change, and your automatic responses will change. You will become a more positive person.

Negativity is not the only limiting enemy that can be engrafted in this way. The same could be said for anger, bitterness, hurt, loneliness, fear, depression, rejection, inferiority, and on and on the list could go. If this is true for you, be mindful that these things have the power to determine the quality of your life and the boundaries of your future.

Our challenge is to revolutionize our soul by exchanging negative qualities for powerful and positive attributes such as confidence, boldness, peace, happiness and prosperity. Cultivate your soul with these qualities and they will become the ingredients that determine your life.

This inward change produces outward change, not vice versa.

HEARING VERSES DOING AND ACHIEVING

There are many people who HEAR about destiny but never experience it. They may have read or heard about the power of change, but have never facilitated or realised it in their own life.

Perhaps you have heard about success and prosperity. Perhaps you have hoped for abundance, and even worked hard, but your expectation has not yet materialised. When transformation begins to take place in your soul, you will become a DOER and fruit will become evident in your life. You will begin to achieve and success won't just be something you hear about in someone else's life.

Henry Ford once said "You can't build a reputation on what you are going to do." Perhaps you have read a lot of books and heard a lot of speakers but if all you do is HEAR motivating words and listen without applying the messages to your life, you are not being a wise steward.

WISDOM IS APPLIED KNOWLEDGE

Applied knowledge produces wisdom in our life. A person may look into a mirror and catch a glimpse of their potential. They may be able to recognise a tangible opportunity, but unless they make an active commitment to pursue such, they will never actually secure these things.

"Don't wait for your ship to come in . . . swim out to it."

Your life is a product of what is in your soul. It

does not depend on knowing the right people or being at the right place at the right time. It's not a lucky break that builds your life. Your life is built through a prosperous soul.

Absorb the truth within these wise proverbs;

I trust that you may prosper in all things and be in health just as your **soul** prospers.[12]

These sentiments outline a powerful life principle. Your life cannot prosper if your soul is impoverished and defeated.

A man's **heart** plans his ways . . . [13]

Our heart directs our course more than we realise. If your heart plans negativity, it will determine the way you live - Negatively! If your heart plans according to your Destiny, your dream will become the source from which your life flows. Remember - you have a future. You were designed and created for a life of achievement and happiness.

Keep your **heart** with all diligence for out of it spring the issues of life.[14]

Be disciplined and diligent with regard to your soul. You have to tend it the way a gardener tends his garden: watering, fertilising and removing the weeds that choke potential. Why? Because out from your soul springs self-esteem, self-confidence, positive attitude, faith, perception and hope in the future. Not from a lucky break, rich relative or lottery ticket. Real success flows from your soul.

Have you noticed how many lottery winners end up in disaster? The lucky break they thought was their answer to life's problems, ended up bringing heartache. Was it because their winnings were cursed? Or was it more related to the wisdom of Solomon who observed:

> An inheritance **gained hastily** at the beginning will not be blessed at the end. [15]

The truth is that outward prosperity will soon be sabotaged by a non-prosperous soul.

YOUR SOUL WILL SHRINK IT

If the prosperity you have outwardly is greater than the prosperity in your soul, your soul will quickly reduce it down to size.

It's easy to set some people up in a small business ... get them to run a large business and wait! The size of their business will be determined by the size of their soul.

On several occasions I have seen businesses, organisations and churches make a momentous decision to amalgamate. Initially it seemed that this brought instant prosperity as the new group became two or three times bigger than before. But whether it maintains this instant "success" is determined by the capacity of the leaders. If their souls are smaller than their success, the organisation will soon be shrunk down to the size of their souls. Leaders must position themselves to be enlarged if they wish to see continuing development in their life's pursuits. There are no shortcuts.

What about the lottery winners? Instant riches don't destroy them, their foolishness does. The inability to handle the sudden windfall. This lack of wisdom has been known to wreck marriages, families and friendships and leave people in a far worse financial situation than when they initially received the money.

YOU DECIDE

We are each in control of our own lives. We each decide whether we will connect with our destiny or miss the mark. The thoughts we cultivate in our heart create either success or lack.

"It's not the mountain we conquer, but ourselves." (*Sir Edmund Hillary*)

The problem is not the boss, the hours people work, or the conditions of the job, the problem is the condition of the human heart.

For as a man thinks in his heart, so is he.

A good heart produces good things. An evil heart, evil things. A victorious heart produces victory and a defeated heart produces defeat.

A PROSPEROUS SOUL

Here are some keys to developing a prosperous soul and a prosperous journey.

1.Educate Your Soul

It is not good for a soul to be **without knowledge**.[17]

It amazes me that a person can have a Masters Degree in Psychology and at the same time be dependent on anti-depressant tablets. Another can have a Degree in Communications but get divorced and re-married many times. Someone else can have a Doctorate in Economics but have no idea how to overcome their personal cash flow problems.

Why is this? They are educated, but their soul isn't,

and of course, the soul is the engine room of life.

Perhaps these people need to go to a new school, and teach their soul some truths. Why? It is knowing the truth, not the facts, that sets you free. It is a matter of educating your soul in such a way as to enable it to have ready access to truth.

How well educated your soul is, becomes evident when it is tested. How do you respond to discouragement? What reflexes do you reveal when criticised? How well do you handle stress, criticism or set backs? An educated soul KNOWS very well not to panic, not to react, and not to quit.

2. Anchor Your Soul

A human can live a certain number of days without water, and a little longer without food, but they can't even begin to live without hope. Hopelessness rules in the souls of so many people. It creates incredible insecurity and instability, and it binds and chokes all potential.

If hope anchors the soul, then a person lacking in hope is obviously unanchored. Imagine them floating like a piece of driftwood, they will be at the mercy of every wave and tide, with no direction, and circumstances will dictate where they will go and how they get there.

In your life where do you pin your expectation? Natural skills? Family? Friends? Income and lifestyle? These can all change overnight. Hope, based on sound qualities within the soul, provide a better anchor, a better foundation! A foundation more likely to withstand the storms and circumstances of life.

Champion Australian athlete, Andrew Lloyd, had every reason to lose hope when his wife was killed in a tragic car accident (which also left him a potential cripple). Doctors said he would never run again, and yet he went on to achieve even greater things by becoming a top level track and field athlete.

Miraculously, Lloyd eventually made it into the Commonwealth Games. During his event he lagged by more than half a lap. Andrew's hope, which had carried him from plaster casts and physiotherapy right up to competing against the world's best, never wavered. In a spectacular effort he surged forward and passed the front runners for a gold medal victory!

3. Enlarge Your Soul

To enlarge something usually involves a process of stretching, extending or modifying design, for the purpose of improvement.

Everyone has the capacity to either enlarge or reduce the capacity of their soul. When you think positively about the future, when you learn from your past mistakes, when you take steps forward and change, you are enlarging your soul.

On the other hand, you can also limit or reduce your soul by remaining victim to negative thoughts. Fear of change or another failure can leave you stagnating instead of moving forward in your journey of life.

An enlarged and prospering soul doesn't rely on external factors. It is quietly confident in the goodness of life and the hope it possesses. When you have an enlarged soul you have a stabilising anchor for your life.

4. Make Your Soul Accountable

In the 1970's, George Foreman was the undefeated world heavyweight boxing champion when he fought Muhammed Ali in Zaire, Africa. Many people thought Foreman would be too strong, but he was outwitted and outboxed by Ali. A recent television interview intrigued me. Twenty years on and in his late 40's, George Foreman was still boxing.

The interview recounted a legendary story about the antics of the Ali camp. They had arrived in Zaire well before George Foreman and spent considerable time gaining the support of the locals. When Foreman arrived in Africa, Muhammed Ali's minders had arranged for George's interpreters to mistranslate any interviews. If George said "I am pleased to be in Africa", they interpreted "I hate Africa". By fight time, all of Zaire were on the side of Ali.

In the interview, twenty years later, it was suggested to Foreman that this was a reason behind his defeat. Foreman answered, "It wasn't the crowd's right hand I felt, and it wasn't their left jab." In other words, he wasn't looking for excuses. He knew he was beaten fair and square.

As long as someone is looking for a reason to excuse the way they are, nothing about them will ever change. If they are going to take authority over their soul and see it develop in a way that builds prosperity into every area of their life, then they have to take account for their life.

How long can someone blame their alcoholic father or their constantly nagging mother for the way they feel? When will they stop using their parents' divorce or their school teacher's comments to excuse their attitudes?

That is not to say that these things don't contribute to our make-up to some degree. But how long must we live victim to them? It's time to MAKE THE DECISION to move on from your hang-ups. NO MORE EXCUSES.

There will always be an excuse, if that's what we're looking for. There is always a reason to justify our doubt. As long as we entertain such thoughts, we continue to place limits on our life.

One day your time on earth will end. On that day, you won't be answering for your father and he won't be answering for you. None of us will be able to blame anyone else for wasted opportunity.

We are all accountable for our own lives. Being accountable means to be actively and positively changing our soul: our mind, will and emotions.

It means to guard our thoughts and words, protecting our positive outlook and, as we're about to discover, use our mind and imagination to dream our way toward our destiny.

How do you move on? With the strength that comes from hope and faith in your ability to achieve a fulfilling life. If your soul is defeated it will negatively affect everything.

Your outlook on life is determined by what you are looking out from. The condition of your soul is the determining key. When you recognise that it's not what happens around you but what happens IN you that matters, you can GET A LIFE!

TAKE ACTION

1. **Decide** to change internally.

2. **Refuse** to transfer blame or to deny personal accountability.

3. **Educate** your soul with the truth.

4. **Build** hope into your life and anchor your soul.

5. **Daily exchange** negativity with positive hope and expectation for the future.

6. **Stop** looking for excuses for who you are and where you are. Your future is in your own hands.

CHAPTER FIVE

YOUR DREAM WILL SET THE STAGE FOR LIFE

"All men dream: but not equally. Those who dream by night in the dusty recesses of their minds, wake in the day to find that it was vanity; but the dreamers of the day are dangerous men, for they may **act their dream with open eyes** to make it possible."

T.E. LAWRENCE

(The Seven Pillars of Wisdom)

Characteristics Of A Dreamer

1. Dreamers Will Threaten Some
   People.

2. Dreamers Keep Dreaming
   New Dreams.

3. Dreamers Understand Other
   Dreamers.

The Anatomy Of A Dreamer

1. The Will To Live

2. The Will To Succeed

3. The Will To Serve

YOUR DREAM WILL SET THE STAGE FOR LIFE

A prosperous soul is one which is full of wisdom, is positive and understands its potential. With a prosperous soul you live a prosperous life. A prosperous life is filled with satisfaction. It causes you to live effectively and leads you into your destiny.

The foundation for an incredible destiny is an incredible dream.

Every high rise building begins as a dream on an architect's board. Multinational companies start as a dream in someone's heart. Great social accomplishments, and missionary endeavours are birthed as a dream in somebody's destiny.

"Houston, you're a dreamer!" To some people that's a put-down. To me it's a compliment. "Yes, I am. And proud of it!"

Human nature has an unbelievable capacity to take

the opposite stance to a positive outlook. The human mind is capable of extraordinary thought and boundless imagination. But we mess around with blinkered, short-sighted vision.

> "A man can achieve any dream he is capable of conceiving. The only boundaries we have are the ones we place on our own imaginations." *(Tom De Falco)*

A dream is the foundation for destiny. And destiny is the fulfilment of a dream.

You cannot help admiring someone like Amy Semple-McPherson. In the 1920's she had a dream of building a 5,000 seat dome in Los Angeles. Architects told her it couldn't be built, that it wouldn't stand. Others mocked. Not only did she build it, but she also filled it with thousands of people night after night.

Or Martin Luther King, whose passionate dream to change his country's culture, actually outlived him and remains alive today.

And what about the persistence and single-mindedness of Walt Disney? Bank after bank turned down his plans to transform a swamp area into a theme park with a cartoon mouse, but he never gave up. Today Disneyland is a household name.

When Disney's futuristic EPCOT Centre was opened some time after his death, the comment was made "What a pity Walt was not here to see it." The response was classic: "Walt saw it, that's why it is here!"

> "Imagination is more important than knowledge."
> *(Albert Einstein)*

It is tragic that many people have no dream. Without a dream it is unlikely they will ever reach their destiny or potential.

CHARACTERISTICS OF A DREAMER

So, what does a dreamer look like? How does he or she think? The following are three characteristics that dreamers have in common.

1. Dreamers Will Threaten Some People

In ancient Egypt under the rule of Rameses II, Joseph, the Hebrew son of a farmer, dreamed that he would be a leader. He believed he would rise up above all his peers and lead a nation. He expected his brothers to be excited. Instead, they were jealous and beat him until he was almost dead. Then they threw him in a pit before selling him as a slave.

Dreaming can be a dangerous business! Sometimes the people closest to us react the most violently to our dreams. If you dare to be a dreamer don't expect everybody to like you, or to like your dream. Joseph's siblings did not appreciate their little brother, nor the affection their father had for him, and they clearly despised his dream.

I have a dream related to my life's purpose. This dream inspires me and gives me a reason to get up in the morning. Not everybody is as excited about that dream as I am. As my dream unfolds, my life has developed, my opportunities have increased and my confidence has grown, but this clearly threatens some people. I am not deterred. On the contrary, it only makes me more determined.

2. Dreamers Keep Dreaming New Dreams

Despite being in his seventies I never hear my father, Frank, talk about the good old days, even though he has had plenty to speak of. He has been helping people for over fifty years and his biography *Being*

Frank contains story after story of miracles and adventure. But he continues to dream new dreams. It is little wonder that he is still excited with life, and continues to travel the world speaking and helping others. What's more, he believes his best days are yet to come. His capacity to dream keeps him inspired and motivated.

> "The ultimate defence against growing old is your dream. Nothing is as real as a dream. Your dream is the path between who you are and the person you hope to become. Success isn't money. Success isn't power. The criteria for your success are to be found in your dream, in yourself. Your dream is something to hold on to. It will always be the link with the person you are today, young and full of hope. If you hold on to it, you **may grow old, but you will never be old**. And that is the ultimate success." (*Tom Clancy*)

3. Dreamers Understand Other Dreamers

Joseph, the Hebrew boy, found himself interpreting the dreams of two of Pharaoh's servants while he was in prison. Joseph ended up being the only person Pharaoh would trust to interpret his own dreams. Being a dreamer himself, Joseph understood and this meeting with other dreamers released him into the fulfilment of his own dream. He also saved an entire nation from starvation in the process. Joseph's ability to keep his dream alive, despite extreme opposition, delivered his destiny.

When you dream a big dream, other dreamers will inspire and encourage you to hold on to it and to keep dreaming new dreams.

THE ANATOMY OF A DREAMER

If your dream is going to become destiny you need to understand the make-up, or character, of the dreamer. Three things are required in order for your dream to become reality:

1. The Will To Live

2. The Will To Succeed

3. The Will To Serve

Practically everybody has the will to live because self-preservation comes naturally. Not quite so many have the will to succeed because there is a cost involved. Even fewer have the will to serve because our culture is geared towards self gratification. Perhaps this is the reason many people never see their dream become reality.

The will to live is not enough. Life is more than mere existence. Destiny suggests a greater purpose and so therefore we must live to succeed. However success in itself is also not enough. Success without a higher purpose becomes self-centred and is therefore limited in impact and can corrupt the soul. The will to serve sets the perfect stage. Let's develop these thoughts further.

1. The Will To Live

Life is a choice. Many people are breathing but they're not living. Breathing existence, surviving, or maintaining do not represent a full life.

To choose life not only affects you, but can affect the course of the generations following you. Your dream can breathe life into your existence, build your destiny but also change the course of future generations. However, you are going to need the will to live because there are plenty of volunteers eager to kill your dream.

Experience proves that certain attitudes can be labelled "Dream Killers". The following life-ailments will suck life from your dream if left unchecked.

i. Failure to Continue To Learn and Grow

"The wise man is not the man who gives the right answers; he is the one who **asks** the right questions." (*Charles Levi-Strauss*)

Life is a learning process and our commitment to growing in knowledge should never stop. If you get to the place where you "can't be told", you risk killing your dream. The day you think "there's nothing more to learn" is a dangerous day.

An insecure person does not like to be told what to do or how to do it. You can learn something from every experience in life, but sadly there are many people who never do learn the lessons.

King Solomon said it this way:

A wise man will hear and increase learning, and a man of understanding will attain wise counsel.

Give instruction to a wise man, and he will be still wiser; teach a just man and he will increase in learning.[18]

There is always room for development. The beauty of a dreamer is that as they walk out their dream, and move towards its fulfilment, they are always hungry to learn, always observing life. Every experience in life presents an opportunity to learn - success, failure, other people, frustration, impossibility, disappointment and breakthrough.

Everywhere I go, I watch, observe and listen. Life is an education. The more I know, the more I can achieve. And the more I know, the more I realise there is still more to know, meaning there will always be more I can achieve.

"Living is a continuous learning process. The world is a fascinating place and the more you find out the more you want to find out!" (*Patricia Wennerstrom*)

ii. Acceptance of Natural Limitations

Dreams are not built on maintaining the status quo. There will always be someone to tell you why it can't be done and why you can never achieve it.

A dreamer lives at a different level. They envisage a life beyond the possible and aim for the impossible. They understand the difference between conforming and transforming. We are surrounded by pressure to conform, to set our thinking to the level of our environment. Transformation is about change. It is a determination to change our circumstance by changing the way we think.

We need to continually elevate our thinking. If we want to live a higher way, we must think higher thoughts. Narrow thinking produces nothing.

Success comes from new ways and new levels of thought. Transform the blandness of a mediocre life into the fruitfulness of a fulfilled dream.

The possibilities for potential will never fit into the confines of flawed humanity, nor the limitations of normal thinking.

iii. Willingness To Bow To Reason

> There is a way that SEEMS right to a man but its end is the way of DEATH. [19]

To reason is to argue what seems reasonable or what seems right. For example:

> It may SEEM right to a teenager growing up in a town with massive unemployment, to settle for a life without a job.

> It may SEEM right to a fifth generation coalminer, to believe that a life in the mines is his only choice.

> It may SEEM right to a young couple battling with two jobs just to pay the rent and survive, never to expect a home of their own. . .

But what SEEMS right will spell death to a dreamer's destiny. A dream will never SEEM right to a "reasonable" man. Author George Bernard Shaw wrote:

> "The reasonable man adapts himself to the world; the unreasonable one persists in trying to adapt the world to himself. Therefore, all progress depends on the unreasonable man."

Reasoning can be limited by perception. It can base its decision on what is known and can fear the unknown. It then accepts the achievable rather than exploring the world of the unachievable. Reason inevitably has the power to cut short our potential. Dare to stretch yourself beyond the boundaries and inhibitions of reason and believe to accomplish something quite unreasonable.

A few short years ago I met a teenage boy full of dreams about business and making money. He talked a lot and had even invested in some far-flung idea such as growing pineapples in Fiji. It didn't SEEM possible that his dreams would amount to very much more than talk.

Ten years on, he is now a successful businessman, husband and father who contributes tens of thousands of dollars into great causes each year. It was unreasonable to expect that this young man from a hurt and broken family background, could accomplish so much in so little time. Such scepticism however, did not deter him.

> "Failure is not failure to meet your goal. Real failure is failure to reach as high as you possibly can."
> (*Dr Robert Schuller*)

iv. Refusal to Discipline Your Words

Death and life are in the power of the **tongue**.[20]

Words have a dynamic and creative power. Few people realise the power behind the words they speak. If a dreamer is to see their vision become reality, they have to be committed to speaking words of life.

"I can't...",

"It's too hard...",

"We'll never make it..."

"This is impossible..."

All these things speak death to your dream. The Proverbs are filled with excellent counsel related to your speech. Observe the following verses:

The mouth of the wise is a well of **life**.[21]

Is your mouth a well of life or a swamp of defeat?

Death and life are in your tongue's power. If you're unable to speak positive words of life when it comes to the dreams of others, it is most unlikely you will see life in your own vision or dream. Cynicism and sarcasm are a reflection of the condition of the heart. Criticism and negativity reveal the inner condition of the one who expresses it. If you genuinely desire your dream to become destiny, you must train yourself to speak words that are breathing life into your dream, and avoid any conversation which is swamping or cutting off that dream.

He who restrains his lips is wise. [22]

Minimum Words, Maximum Impact. Watch out for these potential thieves - overtalking and underachieving. Your dreams will never be realised simply by talking about them.

I try to avoid making rash statements about what I am going to achieve. Actions speak louder than words and I have seen far too many people lose credibility through rash and impulsive statements. Even though they may see healthy increase over a given period, if it falls short of their prediction to a noticeable degree, the impact is lost and demotivation often takes over.

"Some people dream of worthy accomplishments, while others stay awake and do them."

A few years ago I sat at a table with two friends and after a healthy meal, we began to talk about the future. The first man spoke about grandiose plans and ideas. He was quick to tell us what he was going to do, but there was no evidence of a strategy. The other had far less to say, but there was clear evidence that he had thought his future through. He was focused and quietly determined. Today, the latter of these two men is right on track fulfilling his dream, but the former is still only talking about it.

The wise are inwardly determined but know when to restrain their lips. As the saying goes:

Loose lips sink ships *and* Talk is cheap

but ...

The lips of the wise feed many

Generosity begins with the way you speak. Are your lips committed to feeding others and feeding your own dream? Potential requires words of life and encouragement. Abundant and generous words which feed the inner man. Remember that generosity is the currency for success.

If people were to receive their sustenance from encouraging words others spoke to them, a vast majority would be malnourished.

The average American father spends less than ten minutes speaking to his children each day. Obviously, these children are not on a rich diet of encouragement.

A strong leader must be committed to "feeding" the dreams of others, but also watch that your own dreams are not suffering the side effects of starvation.

The lips of the wise know what is acceptable. [23]

Negativity, cynicism, gossip, abuse and criticism. These are unacceptable to your dream and should not be acceptable to your lips.

You may remember the 1980's pop song by Bony-M that echoed another wise proverb. "Let the words of my mouth and the meditation of my heart be ACCEPTABLE in your sight ..."

You cannot separate the words of your mouth from the meditation of your heart. Each feeds the other, and both must be acceptable. The words which are acceptable are those which enhance your dream.

v. An Uncontrolled Lifestyle

"Character is what a man is in the dark." (*D.L. Moody*)

A lifestyle out of control spells DEATH to a dream. There are so many tragic stories of people who have sabotaged their destiny for the sake of a temporary distraction or pleasure.

If your dream is going to produce the abundant life that awaits you, you need to build and establish correct disciplines.

Martin Luther King Jnr was quoted as saying:

"The time is always right to do what is right."

Joe Weider is known as the father of modern day body building. He impresses me, not for his muscles, but for his philosophy on life. The one thing we must always understand about a healthy attitude to discipline, is that it is not designed to diminish or take away from life. It enhances life.

"Strive for excellence, exceed yourself, love your friend, speak the truth, practise fidelity and honour your father and mother. These principles will help you master yourself, make you strong, give you hope and put you on the path to greatness." (*Joe Weider*)

Many motivational speakers and authors can convey philosophies and advocate principles. The problem is, that if they don't live by the principles they promote, they will accomplish nothing. Principles alone aren't enough. They have to translate into lifestyle. You may think that your *personal life* and *business life* are not related, but history teaches otherwise. Much potential has been devastated when individuals refuse to grow or change personality and character weaknesses.

> "There is no real excellence in all this world which can be separated from **right living**." (David Starr Johnston)

vi. Lack of Vision

> "They can because they think they can." (Virgil (Aenid) 70-90 B.C.)

> Without vision the people perish. [24]

Helen Keller was born both deaf and blind, yet she became a tremendous inspiration to people all over the world when she overcame her limitations and lead a fulfilled life. Helen was once asked if she could think of anything worse than being blind. Her reply was very powerful, "Yes, having eyes but not being able to see."

Her dream to converse became the most important goal in her life because although she didn't have natural sight, she did have vision.

> Long life to your dreams! Happy is the man who finds wisdom ... Length of days are in (wisdom's) right hand. [25]

The will to live is a commitment to longevity. A life of tomorrows, not just today. If you have a big dream you will need a long life to see it completed. I have not accomplished all my hopes and dreams. I plan to live a long life and I plan to be active in these pursuits, till the day I die.

Longevity is not just a physical thing. Many people peak at one point in their life and spend the rest of their years living in decline, in the past. For example, the sportsman who spends his days in the club telling long and detailed stories about the "good old days" constantly comparing the athletes of today with those of his own era, is not living.

Life should not climax at some point, boast "I've made it!", and waste the rest of its time reminiscing about yesteryear. True life winds upwards, getting better every day. Mere existence isn't my idea of a long and fruitful life. Dependence on past support systems isn't my idea of living.

The will to live is more than physical. It breathes life into your dreams and gives them a long season.

Our minds have a great capacity to glorify and embellish the past. Happily, we can avoid this inclination when we dream about the future.

THE END SHOULD ALWAYS BE BETTER THAN THE BEGINNING! A dream is only a starting point. It stands in the present, looking into the future and captures a glimpse of where you will end up. It represents your desire, aspirations and vision. You will secure this end, by having a commitment to wisdom and disciplined living.

Many people start well, but allow lack of control and lack of discipline to wreck their opportunities. Never wonder where your life will end, if you're not living right. It is very clear that it will finish in frustration, disappointment, unreached goals and wasted potential.

Joseph's dream had to outlive many potential dream killers. He endured discouragement, temptation, impatience, harsh and unfair treatment and many other potentially fatal blows.

He was placed in a situation where a beautiful woman gave him every opportunity to sacrifice his destiny for an adulterous liaison.

Impatience could easily have beaten Joseph when circumstances continually distanced him from his dream.

Did anyone ever have more reasons to give up than Joseph? He was beaten, sold, used, tempted, betrayed, jailed. However, his dream protected his destiny and helped keep his course.

This dream also kept him on course, even when the course didn't seem fair. It was unreasonable. And when excess could have sabotaged his impact as leader in Egypt, good management initiated by Joseph, meant that the nation had stored up supplies for the time of famine.

Joseph applied wisdom to his life, transforming it from humble and negative beginnings, to become a rich and glorious success!

A dreamer must be committed to staying on course without being tempted, distracted or discouraged. They must stay focused on the goal. They must not allow the pollution of compromise, mediocrity or low standards to get in their way. This is accomplished by the will to live and the desire to keep your dream alive.

2. The Will to Succeed

Joseph's boyhood dream of success was a principal key to his achieving this success. He was a success in Potiphar's house. He succeeded in interpreting dreams. Ultimately, this young man became a very successful leader at the age of 30!

In fact Joseph became so successful that "all countries" came to buy his grain. He was immensely wealthy, extremely popular, and very powerful.

Is success wrong? No.

Is it possible for you to succeed? Definitely.

Is success necessary? Absolutely!

A negative outlook, which is so prevalent in today's society, can have a restrictive and demotivating effect on people to the point where success is regarded by "some people" as being almost immoral and indicative of evil.

This negative outlook makes the person focus on the abuse and misuse of a minority. They incorrectly conclude therefore, that success represents selfishness and greed. The truth is, such a person is failing to recognise a greater purpose than themselves or the responsibility to personally succeed, and so they reject the prosperous life available to them. Rather, they tend to lean toward a 'welfare' mentality, that varies according to the degree of their negativity.

The will to live is not enough on its own because life is more than mere existence. You can't ignore your greater purpose, and mediocrity will never fulfil it. Success should not even an option. It is your responsibility, and to ignore the above is to court living way below your created potential.

To glorify mediocrity is a tragedy. The sad fact is that far too many people make choices which flatly reject success and prosperity.

Religion has often been guilty of this, and yet the gospel is GOOD NEWS. The good news is ABUN-DANT LIFE. Abundance means plentiful.

- Adam was told to be fruitful and multiply.

- Joshua was challenged to make his way prosperous and have good success.

- Solomon's writings are filled with promised prosperity as the fruit of wisdom.

- Jeremiah believed it and prophesied "a future and a hope".

- Jesus spoke about one hundredfold return, telling many stories and parables that encouraged us to multiply our talents.

- The apostle Paul reminded us that though Jesus was rich He took poverty upon Himself. Why? So that YOU through His poverty might be rich.

- The apostle John wished prosperity and good health on his friend.

Never excuse mediocrity by rejecting success. It is within our "created fibre" to succeed. However, it is a success committed to serving and making a difference. To impacting and influencing, building and giving and establishing good on earth. For that reason a dreamer must not only dream to succeed, but also dream to serve.

3. The Will To Serve

"Only a life lived for others is a life worthwhile." *(Albert Einstein)*

At every stage of Joseph's life he was committed to serving, and in doing so he became a successful prime minister who brought great blessing to his nation.

- What great cause does your dream serve?

- Where is it likely to make a difference?

The will to serve does not necessarily mean that you spend all of your days doing servile things. I know people who lead huge organisations and employ many staff, yet they are serving, in that their commitment and their vision extends far beyond themselves. They may have someone to answer their calls or drive them to the airport, yet they themselves are servants or facilitators of a great cause.

Life is not about hoarding and gathering, neither should it represent excess or greed. The will to serve is a commitment to bless others. It may mean seeing how much one can give away in a lifetime, whether it be money or knowledge, time or encouragement.

You were born to live, you live to succeed, you succeed to serve. That is how dreams become impacting reality.

"Half the world is on the wrong scent in the pursuit of happiness. They think it consists in having and getting . . . On the contrary, it consists in giving and in serving . . ." (Henry Drummond)

The will to live, to succeed and to serve were the ingredients in Joseph's character that turned his dream into reality. Become a powerful dreamer!

GET A LIFE!

TAKE ACTION

1. Make it a **constant habit** every day of your life to dream big dreams (frighten yourself!).

2. **Hold on** to your dreams. **Guard against** the Dream Killers.

3. Approach life with the **determination to** turn your dreams into reality.

4. **Choose** a life of service. **Invest** into others to make this a better world.

5. **Be disciplined** in all areas.

6. **Think long-term**. Don't look for short cuts.

OVERCOMERS MEET THE CHALLENGE OF LIFE

"You're not finished when you're defeated . . .

you're finished **when you quit.**"

VAN CROUCH

Finish What You Start

1. An Overcomer Stays Alert.

2. An Overcomer Never Gives Up.

3. An Overcomer Knows Their Season is Coming.

4. An Overcomer Is Committed To Results.

The Necessary Qualities Of An Overcomer

1. A Willing Mind.

2. Work With What You Have.

3. Commitment To Abundance.

OVERCOMERS MEET THE CHALLENGE OF LIFE

FINISH WHAT YOU START

The world is filled with good starters. Pioneer a new venture, announce a study course, call for new leaders and people will line up. But how many of them finish well? Or finish at all?

You must be committed to completing the good things which you have begun in your life. There are many things wanting to hold you back from the vast possibilities of life. Things which could easily hinder every chance you have of reaching your goal or living a quality lifestyle.

- What were you desiring to do a year ago with your life?

- Is your dream as focused now as it was then?

- What desires were in your heart five years ago?

- Or ten years ago?

- Are you still on course?

- Have you changed direction? Are you still pursuing those ambitions in the face of opposition?

- Or have you allowed yourself to be dissuaded or discouraged?

Winners commit to completing these things. Their goals increase, not diminish, and their determination grows stronger as they just keep climbing back up after every knockdown.

Perhaps you feel this is easier said than done. And perhaps that is why there is more said than done! The key is to take on the spirit of an overcomer with the tenacity and perseverance which refuses to give up.

Have you ever watched an Olympic equestrian event? Horses are expected to jump obstacles of various shapes, sizes and degree of difficulty. Imagine if the rider, representing their country in front of a huge crowd and television audience of millions, was to give up at the first hurdle. Perhaps their horse clips the wooden fence and the top beam tragically falls to the ground. Of course they're not going to give up. They continue tenaciously until the last obstacle is passed and the finish line is reached. Tenacity is an essential ingredient for overcomers.

Be assured, your dream will be tested and challenged, but testing is never wasted if it is approached correctly. It can produce incredible insight and become a catalyst for positive and progressive change.

It was Voltaire who was quoted as saying "Everything is for the best, in the best of all possible worlds" (Candide 1759).

A spirit of endurance will turn problems and challenges around to accomplish something positive. It will strengthen you and challenge you to discover resourcefulness and staying-power that you thought you never had, and in doing so you will continue to develop and succeed.

We all need tremendous resources to complete what we have started. People, finance, time, energy and commitment. The ability to endure is essential.

Endurance requires patience and the patience of an overcomer is not passive or weak. Neither is it idle.

- It's TENACIOUS.

- It's COURAGEOUS.

- It's FOCUSED.

- It is both DELIBERATE and DETERMINED.

It holds on against the tide, against public opinion and against the circumstances.

People limit their effectiveness when they lack this overcoming spirit. Some people believe that "successful people" live in a perfect world where there are no challenges, no difficulties and nothing to overcome. Sadly, this incorrect belief can end up in disillusionment and cynicism because unrealistic attitudes leave no room for challenges or problems. Subsequently, when confronted with opposition, such people are found unprepared and ill equipped.

There will always be challenges, but that is what gives life its adventure! Why did Sir Edmund Hillary take the time to plan, build a team, work against the elements and make it to the top of the world's highest mountain, venturing where no man had ever been before? Would he have bothered to put his flag on the summit of Mt Everest were it flat? Of course not!

Hillary wasn't concerned about what he didn't have. He had confidence in what he could do. He came from a small country of just three million people. His native New Zealand didn't have the resources or financial support of the world's superpowers to send a team to climb Everest. Yet he dared to believe that he could do it. And he did.

I once heard the story of a British mountain- climbing team which unsuccessfully attempted to scale Everest. A second team was formed which also failed. Unwilling to give up, the organisers then invited the world famous expedition leader, Mallory, to lead a third team. Tragically, in their attempt they were all killed in an avalanche. The organisers held a gathering back in Britain to eulogise their fallen comrades, and behind the podium was a picture of the mighty peak.

During the service one of the speakers turned his back to the audience and began speaking to that picture on the wall, "We've tried once and you beat us, we've tried twice and failed, we've tried a third time, but Mount Everest, you can't get any bigger **but we can**!"

What does it take to develop this tenacious spirit? What does an overcomer look like?

1. An Overcomer Stays Alert

An overcomer will keep himself or herself fresh. It doesn't take much to discourage some people. Tiredness and weariness may mean that resistance may go down, and a person may become much more susceptible to giving up. However, this is not the tiredness and weariness that results from physical fatigue, a late night or a big day. It is a weariness of heart that develops because of continual striving, and/or discouragement. Nothing is ever accomplished without hard work, but balance is essential.

> "Patience and time do more than force and rage." (*Jean De Fontaine* 1621-16-95)

An overcomer needs to look out for tell-tale signs. Are the things that once inspired you becoming more mundane? Or Boring? Are your energy resources down? Are you getting sick more often? Are you becoming more quick-tempered? Or has kicking the dog become an evening ritual?

Hard work is not actually the problem. Humans are actually designed to work hard, but striving will wear you down. An overcomer will read the signs and make the necessary adjustments to stay fresh.

I love watching my sons play sport. I mix with the other parents, get absorbed in the game, and for me this is stimulating. It's refreshing. For you it may be a game of golf, a bike ride or a quiet cappuccino.

Recreational activity helps you avoid becoming lethargic and weary. It also balances your perspective and encourages creative thought. Do whatever it takes to stay big enough and energised enough to conquer your "mountains."

2. An Overcomer Never Gives Up

It's no use being the fastest, if you don't actually finish the race. The reward is on the finish line.

Many people do well for a period of time. They're focused and making progress but over time (and for whatever reason) they slow down and/or give up. Overcomers continue. The key is that they remain active, they persist in actualising or "doing" what they set out to do.

People love to instruct or give advice, but overcomers are DOERS. An overcomer not only has good ideas and intentions, but follows through with action.

I guess it's like comparing a "crash diet" with a "healthy lifestyle of diet and exercise". The first will help you squeeze into your swimwear for next summer, but the moment you stop the diet programme, back come the kilos with a vengeance! The second is an active commitment to establish and continue with the good habits, in order to achieve the desired long-term results.

Overcomers keep on keeping on.

"Success is largely a matter of holding on after others have let go." (*Anonymous*)

3. An Overcomer Recognises Their Season Is Coming

Everything in life points to seasons. In the '60's, The Seekers sang "there is a season . . . a time for every purpose under heaven".

Has it ever seemed as though no matter how hard

you try or how long you wait, the breakthrough just won't come? Don't despair! Sometimes we can feel like we'll never see the light at the end of the tunnel, but you will as long as you STAY ON the train. Don't jump off in the tunnel!

In fact it may feel as though your season is not only due, but well overdue. HOLD ON FOR YOUR SEASON especially if you are confident of having done everything right, because after every winter comes spring and after every sunset comes sunrise.

"Accept the challenges so that you may feel the exhilaration of victory." (*George S. Patton*)

4. An Overcomer Is Committed To Reaping

Sowing and reaping are a law of life. You may have heard the statement:

They that sow in tears shall reap in joy. [26]

However, all the crying, sobbing, griping, whingeing, howling, screaming, sulking and grinding of teeth that you can muster, will not make you reap a quality life. So, what will?

Crying won't help you unless it is accompanied with continual sowing of the right seed. Don't stop at the weeping, as it is unproductive on its own. To be the overcomer you desire to be, you must continue to sow good seed. Refuse to throw in the towel. Refuse to quit.

"People who have attained things worth having in this world have worked while others have idled, have pursued when others gave up in despair ..." (*Grenville Kleiser*)

For you, sowing may be knocking on doors or sell-ing an idea. Perhaps it's making more calls, investing more money or helping more people, but you will never reap the rewards and benefits of true success without first having a commitment to sowing.

So What Happens Next?

You have seen what an overcomer looks like, but how do you get there? How do you reverse the natu-ral tendency to start well, do good for a season and then give up short of the finish line?

Can you remember when your dreams and desires for the future began to stir inside you and kept you awake at night? Maybe you were inspired to start an endeavour or build a business. Perhaps you were committed to a course of study or challenged to over-seas service. What does it take to see that vision be-come reality?

Remember, the answer is found in completing what you start.

THE NECESSARY QUALITIES OF AN OVERCOMER

Here are three qualities of an effective overcomer. These qualities strengthen and equip you to meet life's challenges and are easily applied to life.

1. A Willing Mind

Do a check-up from the neck up!

There are many forces that want to play with your head. Sadly many people are victims of "stinking thinking". If your mind is not cooperating with your goals, then you are not going to see them completed.

There is a process to destructive thinking. An unchecked thought has the potential to engulf and overtake your life.

In early Greek history, residents of Corinth were taught four progressive levels of destructive thinking which remain valid :

(i)   Thoughts

(ii) High Thoughts

(iii) Arguments

(iv) Strongholds

Now watch how they work.

i. Thoughts

Your THOUGHTS can determine your future. At times our minds produce negative patterns of thinking which need to be arrested. We can't allow these THOUGHTS to roam free, they should be locked up. They are a menace, so constrain them and refuse to allow your mind to wander down destructive paths.

ii. High Thoughts

Contrary to accepted belief, your mind doesn't control you, you control it. Therefore you need to be in total control of your thoughts. Failure to do this takes you to the second level where these thoughts become preoccupations or HIGH THOUGHTS. They now preoccupy you and dominate your thinking. Remember:

As a man thinks in his heart so is he. [27]

You'll build or devastate your life according to your thinking.

Some powerful dynamics are at play here, so absorb the progression happening here.

iii. Arguments

If you still do not take authority over such thinking, it becomes an ARGUMENT, which comes from the Greek word "logismos" meaning logical thinking or philosophical reasoning. In other words, it starts making sense to you.

When reason and destructive thinking make more sense to you, than the dream birthed in your heart, your dream is in trouble, and so are you!

iv. Strongholds

Eventually an unchecked thought becomes a STRONGHOLD which will then need to be pulled down. Because strongholds are just that; they take a strong hold over your mind and subsequently, have a strong hold, or a vice-like grip, on your destiny.

"Thoughts" become "high thoughts", or preoccupying and dominating thoughts. "High thoughts" become "arguments". They resist wisdom and challenge an overcomer's spirit. Then these "arguments" become "strongholds" which depose the wisdom of overcoming.

The major focus for this chapter is the importance of completing what you have begun. This involves much more than being a good starter. It is a commitment to being a great finisher.

There are enemies which will build destructive strongholds around your mind and stop you in your tracks.

Look at the following examples:

• Stronghold 1: Impoverished Thinking

This stronghold will keep you feeling poor. And poor is a way of thinking. You could be broke but not poor. Conversely, you can have great wealth and yet be poor because poverty is a state of mind. This depends on your attitude. For example, John Paul-Getty is reputed to have said "I have enough money to own every heifer cow in America but my stomach is so full of ulcers that I cannot even enjoy one steak."

Many people live under the stronghold of believing poverty is their fate and that there is nothing they can do to change it. If nothing is done to change such thinking, it is guaranteed to limit your life to the level of your belief.

• Stronghold 2: Ignoring advice

When negativity has become a stronghold, the last thing you want is advice. You don't want anybody telling you what to do, or how to do it. The oppressive thoughts that rule you, will confuse "concern and advice" for interference. You then potentially isolate yourself, and cut yourself off from any positive input.

"When a man is wrapped up in himself, he makes a pretty small package." (*John Ruskin*)

• Stronghold 3: The Disadvantages

Can you still see the advantages or benefits that belong to your life's dream? Or have disadvantages and unfavourable conditions blocked your view? Lack of initial reward, challenges, or the cost that accompanies the commitment, can all become strongholds if not managed correctly.

• Stronghold 4: Giving Up

There have been many occasions when during an early morning jog, the thought of quitting or starting to walk enters my mind. If I don't take that thought captive, it will go through the process of becoming a stronghold.

When I start thinking that way, my legs hurt more, the completion of my run seems a long way off and every argument my mind can muster, makes slowing down to a walk look more attractive. This is exactly how strongholds work.

They have you wanting to give up too soon. They will make the finish line seem too distant to continue. Strongholds will build "stinking thinking" which refuses to cooperate, and thought processes that make you unwilling to continue.

• Stronghold 5: A Victim Mentality

A stronghold has the incredible habit of making you believe that you are the only person with burdens or problems. You may sit in a crowd of people and it seems everyone but you, has got it easy. You may be ruled with thoughts like: "I am the only one with problems," "Everyone else is so happy," or "They've all got their act together."

However I have been in the people business long enough to know that all humanity has challenges. You are never the only one. Far from it. If the victim mentally starts to raise it's ugly head, lose it quickly.

2. Work With What You Have

We become so good at focusing on what we do not have:

"But I don't have the training"

"I haven't got the finance"

"I can't find the time"

"I haven't got the right people"

"I don't have enough support to get it done!"

A leader holds a meeting. Looking out across his audience he focuses on the empty seats in the room, or notices the one person in the back row, scowling at him with his arms folded. Driving home after the meeting, he'll begin to recount on who was missing. The people who weren't there dominate his thinking more than the faithful people who were there.

All employers are aware of the limitations in their staff but it's no use smarting over the one employee who left the company three years ago.

Don't invite such discouragement into your world. Why doesn't the leader see the seats that were filled and the great people who sat in them? Why can't he focus on the great majority of people who were energetically participating, rather than the sad sack in the back row? The reason is because this person is ruled by what they DO NOT HAVE.

You will never build your life's purpose by focusing on what you DON'T HAVE. Begin to see and appreciate WHAT YOU DO HAVE, (and of course strategise to keep moving forward.)

Helen Keller was deaf, dumb and blind and yet

she did not focus on her incredible inadequacies. Her attitude leaves us without excuse: "I am only one, but still I am one. I cannot do everything, but still I can do something; I will not refuse to do the something I can do."

Learn to actively focus on what you do have. Perhaps skills, health, family, friends and definitely a future. Where there is life, there is always hope!

A 'sense of lack' has the capacity to work against some positive qualities. Lack is:

(i)   contrary to faith;

(ii) denies prosperity;

(iii) destroys confidence

(iv) pollutes friendships

i. Contrary To Faith

Faith brings things to life. If you only see what you DON'T HAVE, you're giving faith no working platform in your life. Faith is like fuel to your hopes and dreams and without it they will never be realised.

ii. Lack Denies Generosity

When we get locked into what we DON'T HAVE we begin to skimp and hold back rather than sow and give liberally. This thinking diminishes rather than expands us.

iii. Lack Destroys Your Confidence

You do your self-esteem no favour by listing what you DON'T HAVE. I'm certain there will be plenty of things that we could all add to the list, but these do not create the foundation for an overcomer.

There are many things I can't do. I don't have a voice like Pavarotti or Elton John, I can't play the piano (except the first half of Silent Night), and I can't hit a golf ball like Greg Norman. So what?

I do have the qualities I need to fulfil my purpose for my life, and I recognise that many of these qualities started as seeds and had to be nourished and developed. I choose to be confident in *me:* that is what will build my potential.

What I do not have and cannot do, is irrelevant, and concentrating on it won't build anything; quite the reverse.

iv. Lack Pollutes Relationships

The worst thing a couple can do for their marriage is to try to build it on what they DON'T HAVE. If a man looks at his wife and all he can see is flaws and imperfections, he is undermining his relationship and is a candidate for unfaithfulness.

When a woman looks at her husband and makes negative comparisons with others, she is courting dangerous ground. Be thankful for what you DO have. The basis of a good relationship is to *build* around the positives.

3. Commitment To Abundance

The life of an overcomer is a life moving forward, committed to an overflow of resources. Such abundance should not be an optional extra to aspire to. Rather, understand your success enables you to help others and so live an unselfish, giving and valuable life.

Let's examine two key words:

- SUFFICIENT and

- ABUNDANCE.

Sufficient is for you and abundance is an overflow for the benefit of others. Together, they give you a reason to complete the vision you have begun to pursue.

When someone says "All I need is sufficient for my table", who are they thinking about? Themselves. They are only concerned with their table. With an abundance they could help others by giving them a full table. If someone only wants a car that can get them from A to B what will they do if their life's purpose requires them to go to C, D, E, F or G? They are only wanting sufficient. To want "just enough" is to be only thinking about yourself.

An overcomer does not allow themself the option of giving up, falling short or getting by. That is because their purpose in life is greater than just themself. They recognise the opportunities abundance brings, enabling them to fulfil a higher purpose.

It's not how well you start in life that counts. It's how well you finish. Overcomers take up the challenge of life and complete it. GET A LIFE!

TAKE ACTION

1. Think about your vision and dream. Are you **still pursuing it** ? If not, list those things which have contributed to blurring your vision.

2. **Revive the dr eam** in your heart, make it clear again. (Write it down)

3. **Adjust** your thinking from the disadvantages you have listed above and see the advantages.

4. Don't allow yourself to **grow wear y**. Run a marathon not a sprint. Enjoy a cappuccino along the way!

5. **Focus on what you have** , not on what you don't have.

6. Have a **commitment to abundance** and determine the motivating factors which will continue to inspire you to finish your course.

PROGRESS IS THE GOAL OF LIFE

"A man of destiny knows that beyond this hill **lies another** and another.
The journey is never complete."

F.W. DE KLERK

Progress Is A Process

Four Vital Elements of Progress

1. Be Prepared For The Journey

2. Be Ready To Graduate

3. Beware Of Misguided
   Mindsets and Advice

4. Be Ready For Opportunities

PROGRESS IS THE GOAL OF LIFE

There is a very real difference between momentum and impetus. Imagine driving your car. If you use the accelerator you are giving your car impetus. Take your foot off the accelerator and the car won't stop immediately - momentum will carry it along for a period of time, but eventually, without impetus, your car will grind to a halt.

To inherit the life intended for us, there needs to be a commitment to progress. Not just the desire to start, but the determination to finish. George Bernard had this kind of determination. When asked about the key to his success he revealed: "When I was young, I observed that nine out of ten things I did were failures. So I did ten times more work."

Progress involves impetus and momentum - impetus comes from within, momentum relies on externals.

The condition of your life today reflects the

impetus you have given it up to this point. (This principle is true, both negatively and positively.)

It is easy to begin coasting in life and for a time nothing appears to change, however if no positive impetus is being applied, momentum is already beginning to diminish. Note the following proverb:

The way of the upright is a highway. [28]

It sounds good and easy. But the quote goes on to add new dimension:

The way of life winds upward for the wise. [29]

Life may be a highway, but there are some unexpected bends and curves. There's another saying that "A bend in the road is not the end of the road . . . unless you fail to make the turn."

If you apply wisdom, and remain focused on progress, you'll come out of those bends winding upwards, not spiralling downwards.

For example you don't throw out all of your books on success because you failed once. You don't settle for a lifetime of unemployment because you were retrenched. You don't get a divorce just because you argued one night. Neither do you settle for a lifetime of poverty just because your bank account is nearly empty.

Wisdom enables us to wind upwards and experience the highway, or "higher way".

Continual impetus however is essential. Perhaps you have progressed part of the way along life's highway and have effectively negotiated some of the twists and curves. What impetus are you applying today? Your tomorrow depends on it!

PROGRESS IS A PROCESS

Progress is a process. Many people want the progress without the process. The glory without the guts. The destiny but not the journey. The key is in realising that success is a journey, not a destination.

Progressive people are PASSIONATE people. Passionate about everything that pertains to their life.

Too many people want progress until they realise a risk is involved or until the need for personal discipline is required. Completion will not come without progress, and destination will not come without the journey.

Who wants to be doing the same things they were a year ago? Perhaps you're thinking the last thing you need is another year like last year. Well then, don't settle for it. Have a renewed commitment to progress, and accept and cooperate with the process that accompanies the progress.

Opportunities don't just "happen." Most of the opportunities that I am enjoying today, are a result of desires and dreams that developed deep inside my heart when I was a small child.

> "If we don't change, we don't grow. If we don't grow, we are not really living. Growth demands a temporary surrender of security. It may mean a giving up of familiar but limiting patterns, safe but unrewarding work, values no longer believed in, relationships that have lost their meaning. As Dostoevsky put it, 'taking a new step, uttering a new word, is what people fear most.' The real fear should be the opposite course." (Gail Sheehy, Author N.Y.)

Many people wander aimlessly through life because

they have little passion and no real desire. Consequently, their lives are limited, lacking in adventure, and are ruled by all the wrong desires.

FOUR VITAL ELEMENTS OF PROGRESS

There are major hindrances to progress that can slow you down or distract any of us from our course in life. However there are some vital precautionary measures we can take in order to avoid such diversions occurring.

1. Prepare for the Journey

*"If you **don't know** where you are going, you will probably wind up somewhere else."* (David Campbell)

Several years ago we left on a Sunday evening to embark on a family holiday in Queensland. The journey to the Gold Coast of 1,000+ kilometres was going well ... for the first 25 kilometres!

I was feeling good after a great day and was contemplating the thought of white sands, crystal-clear surf, hot sunshine, and café latte's, when the peace was disrupted by a loud bang. A tyre had blown out.

I stayed nice and calm while I took all of the suitcases and bags out of the boot (one for me and the kids and 15 for Bobbie!). I was still a model of patience while I jacked up the car and the first three wheel nuts cooperated beautifully ... but the fourth one ... the fourth one was not going to budge!

The wheel brace slipped a couple of times and before long my knuckles were bleeding. I looked down at the nice white shirt I had worn to church that night. It was streaked with grease. My joy was fast disappearing, and I got myself to the point where I believed the passing trucks were purposely driving close to me. As time went on, I started to think that these trucks were turning around and coming back to see just how close they could get. Such was my state of mind.

Suddenly, going back home seemed more attractive than continuing on the other 975 kilometres to the Gold Coast.

Finally the wheel nut moved, the tyre was replaced, and we proceeded on to a great holiday. This story illustrates the problem some people have with life. They want the destination, but they don't want the journey.

When you leave Sydney the first built-up areas you go through include Berowra, Wyong and Ourimbah. These are a long way from the Gold Coast, but if you want to drive there you have to go through them.

Usually you're not very far from home when the kids start "Are we nearly there yet?" The worst thing you can do is give them false hope. Never say there's not a long way to go, unless you want to be hounded for the rest of the trip. In our car I always worked from the opposite philosophy. If there was still 300 kilometres to go and I said "It won't be long" I would be giving my children false hope. In their minds, a couple more minutes and we would be there. A couple more bends and we'd see the ocean. In this instance they would definitely be unprepared for what still lay ahead. We may have come a long way, but there was still a lot of road to travel. Even when we were only a few blocks from our destination I'd tell my youngest there was still a long way to go. That way she had a pleasant surprise when we "suddenly" arrived. "I can see the sea!", she would yell.

Kindergarten is a long way from Year 12. If you want to understand Year 12 Advanced Maths you have to learn at some time, that one and one is two, two and two is four, and four minus three is one.

You can't start at Year 10 English if you never learned to read words like "and", "if" and "that". You move on to "bicycle" and "aeroplane". Before you know it you can read "onomatopoeia" and you move on to "antidisestablishmentarianism".

If you want to lose 20 kilos you might get to the end of the first week and find you have only lost two kilos. There is still a long way to go, but you had to work off the first two kilos before you reach the target of 20!

If a networker has a goal to build an exceptional business, and initially there are only one or two faithful people, they could easily become discouraged. But to build their business they have to start somewhere.

To build anything you have to have a starting point. Every step of the building process is essential to the next.

Know the value of a step! Oliver Wendell Holmes said "The greater thing in this world is not so much where we stand as in what direction we are going."

To be prepared for the journey we need to know the value of a step. It doesn't matter how small or large that step is, as long as it takes you in the direction you are called to go. You can't progress whilst you digress or regress. Any step in the right direction is a step closer to your destination.

Have you ever heard the saying "There is only one way to eat an elephant : bite by bite" ?

You need the strength to stick it out over the long haul - not the grim strength of gritting your teeth, but the strength that endures the unendurable. This strength will equip you for the process of progress.

2. Prepare To Graduate

Now do what you've been taught! SCHOOL'S OUT. DON'T STOP AT STUDYING THE SUBJECT . . . START LIVING IT!

There has never been a more educated generation. Computer programs, a huge range of written, videos and audio resource, conferences and training for all levels. There is so much knowledge available to us. While teaching and training prepares you for progress, it will never initiate progress. You have to start DOING it.

There are those who want to succeed, but have no commitment to action. People can be broadly divided into three groups:

- those who **wonder** what's happening
- those who **watch** what's happening
- those who **make** things happen

Which one are you ? Is your life's walk defective or effective, progressive or regressive? You can go to conferences, listen to teaching tapes, attend study groups and say "I can do it", but there's more to it than that. The knowledge has to become active in our lives to make us effective.

A young man wants to go out with a certain girl. He can't simply watch her, read about her or listen to tapes about her. To win her heart he will have to ask her out, learn a little about romance, maybe open a few car doors. He will need to spend some money, buy her flowers, and buy himself some deodorant. He may shower her with gifts expressing his affection. It will take action and cost him something to win her love.

Progress involves action. In life we never stop learning, but it is essential we start living what we learn. This is wisdom - applying the truth to your life.

I know a man who, at various times, has commenced new businesses. He has thought of a great name to trade under, developed the logo and printed the stationery. He does everything except actually start trading. And the reason for this is simple - fear!

Fear stops people from getting out of school and starting on the process of progress. School is only the preparation for the main event.

What a boring life it would be, if school was all there was. I wouldn't like to have the job of telling my two teenage sons that they were sentenced to a lifetime of high school. The only thing that keeps them motivated for school is the knowledge that they are preparing to succeed in life after school.

Yet there are people who only want to be taught, fed, learn, be taught some more, attend another conference, buy the tapes.

Gaining knowledge is vitally important, but knowledge alone won't make you progress. Progress is in the effective application of that knowledge or truth to your life. Progress means DOING.

3. Beware Of Misguided Mindsets and Advice

Some people take the position of being anti-everything. They are full of criticism and judgement and are ruled by what is wrong. They are committed to opposing, preventing and resisting progress. If you are anti- everything, you are pro-nothing! Progress cannot be built from an anti-position. Being on a committee with such a person is intolerable. They'll present you with every conceivable reason why things can't be done.

There is a pressure which comes from a pseudo-knowledge, know-it-all type of person. This defensive behaviour strives to 'bully' others into to mediocrity. It brow-beats people into feeling unworthy, and always comes from the lowest common denominator. It undermines progress, focuses inward, and produces striving. WHY DO YOU LET YOURSELF BE BULLIED BY IT?

I know of people who are controlled by attitudes from their family or peers, which have the appearance of wisdom, but in reality reject progress. They come from the bottom of the pile and focus on all the reasons "why not". Comments such as "it will cost too much" or "we'll never see you" or "it will never work!" negate endeavour and enthusiasm.

Remember, mediocrity is self-justifying. Don't let yourself be bullied by such thinking. More importantly don't take it on board!

Betty Ford's advice, is "Don't compromise yourself, you are all you've got."

Opposition to progress in your life doesn't usually

come from strangers, but from those who are making unfair comparisons or judging you from the 'sidelines'. Sadly it is often the people who are close to you, who will be threatened by your progress and change. If you maintain a good attitude, things have a way of eventually turning around.

Avoid the intimidating variety of advice that has the appearance of wisdom, but is designed to suppress.

There will always be people who are threatened by your progress, because it confronts and lends no support to the weaknesses and shortcomings in their lives ... in fact it only highlights them! No wonder they felt much more comfortable when there was nothing about you to challenge them!

Develop friendships with people who will want to see you rise up, discover promotion and progress into your true purpose. People who rejoice when they see you enjoying your life. Genuine counsel does not crush you; it builds you up. It doesn't come from the bottom of the pile, it comes from the top. Don't be bullied by an attitude that glorifies the bottom of the pile.

If you are popular and outgoing, someone may comment - "We need character, not charisma." Why does there need to be a choice? Why can't you have character AND a dynamic personality? These qualities are not mutually exclusive! "We need quality not quantity." Why choose? Believe for the best and the most.

The most fun-filled, alive, colourful people in society should be those whose lives are committed to progress. After all, they are the ones who understand the direction and purpose for their life, and that is something highly sought after in these uncertain times.

Commitment to progress is not a negative, it is a positive. True commitment does not restrict, it releases. It is not a reaction, but a springboard to action.

Progress is dependent on people who will live a life that goes further than pointing out the problems. They are committed to the answers.

4. Invite Opportunity

Life is filled with opportunities waiting for you to enjoy. My wife Bobbie and I are living a life filled with opportunity. The opportunity to lead great people. The opportunity to raise great children. The opportunity to enjoy rich and fulfilling friendships. Opportunities to travel. Continual opportunities to expand and pioneer new endeavours.

There will always be challenges and trials - that's life. Despite or even because of these struggles, wonderful opportunities emerge for those with the passion to progress.

There are times when it can seem like others have fantastic opportunities opening up for them, but it feels like those doors remain closed for you. God doesn't have favourites, so why should this be?

Is it luck? Is it coincidence? Maybe it's fate?

Why is it always someone else who seems to be in the right place at the right time? Perhaps you think they have the right connections. They know the right people. "They must have cut corners", you may say "They're just one of those pushy-type people." But that describes an opportunist. OPPORTUNISM will never produce opportunity (more about that in a moment).

So, where does opportunity come from? If it is not luck or coincidence, fluke or fate, what is it? Opportunity belongs to everybody. It belongs to you. Opportunity and progress are allies. When you get a glimpse of exciting opportunities the usual response would be to progress toward them.

Your life should not be lacking in new and fresh opportunities and there are five clearly identifiable steps to living a life which is continually producing them.

i. Desire

The determining question is, how much do you want it? What are you prepared to sacrifice in order to achieve it?

Desire is the starting point for progress and desire has remarkable creative energy. If you build the right desires, they have the capacity to produce good things in your life.

Notice this progression. Desire brings a conception, a birth, and an accomplishment. Unhealthy desires, when they are conceived, give birth to unhealthy action. Action which when accomplished, has destructive consequence.

The seriousness of this advice should never be passed over; but healthy desire also conceives, gives birth and accomplishes. The fruit of positive desire, is positive accomplishment.

Some would argue that our desires have very little to do with the outcome of our life, but its amazing what can be achieved when we want it enough.

Nevertheless, there are those who want to settle

down or get off the treadmill. They want a quieter life. Hassle-free. No stress. No challenge. This will not build the life we've been talking about. Maintenance is monotony and "getting by" is mediocrity. Both attitudes reject progress and limit opportunity.

It is important to realise that progress is a law of life. To fight progress produces stress. You are going against the flow because nothing in life remains stationary. People get upset at progress in cities around the world. They don't want new roads or railways, buildings or facilities.

Obviously, discretion and discernment is needed in planning such things, but the nature of a city is progress. Everywhere there is progress, there is opportunity. Jobs, transportation and extra facilities.

Like abundance and progress, opportunity is not an option.

Remember, we are here for a higher purpose. DESIRE IS THE STARTING POINT FOR OPPORTUNITY!

ii. Decisions

Positive desires precede positive decisions. Right decisions put us in the right position for opportunities to strike.

There are some people who look at my wife Bobbie and me and assert "They just happened to be in the right place, at the right time." This, of course, is true. But it was not a fluke and it was not luck. It started with a desire birthed in me as a little boy to be a leader and speaker.

This desire has opened up many wonderful opportunities for me around the world. However, if the desire had not been there, I never would have made the decisions which created those opportunities in the first place.

As a teenager this desire kept me on course even under the severest temptation and enabled me to make right decisions. Decisions like studying in a Leadership College while my friends were heading for the beach. Decisions which often meant personal sacrifice and living outside of my comfort zone. Decisions which position a person to reap a harvest and enjoy success.

You will stay on the path to opportunities as long as your decisions and positive creative desires line up. When your decisions contradict that desire, it is a different story.

For example, if a person's desire is to be a successful business person, every decision they make helps to determine whether they stay on that course. Decisions which contradict that desire would rob them of opportunity. Decisions as seemingly small, as sleeping in and missing a Business course, can affect opportunity.

There may be many things that we want to blame on bad luck, but which in actual reality come right back to our own decisions.

To illustrate, I think it was Mary Quant who said "there is no such thing as an ugly woman, only lazy ones." In other words, attractiveness is a matter of choice, not luck. Many of the difficulties that you encounter can be traced back to decisions you have made.

iii. Position

One of a footballer's greatest gifts is his sense of position. The best sportsmen are always in the right place at the right time. Just as the ball arrives, he appears in the gap and makes the break which wins the match. He has an uncanny sense of position.

Opportunists find themselves in the wrong places at the wrong time. Like pragmatists, they do whatever is convenient. Opportunists look for shortcuts, but their diminutive thinking will always limit them.

They exchange patience and perseverance with the desire for easy and instant success. Life however, doesn't tend to be like that.

Every decision has a consequence. Every action has a reaction.

Imagine someone who buys a home. After two or three years, having seen no appreciation in its value, they sell it and invest in a get-rich-quick scheme. Immediately after they sell, there is a housing boom and everybody else in the street sees the value of their homes double, while they are sinking in a shonky get-rich-not-quite-as-quick-as-I-thought scheme. Wrong decisions put the buyer in the wrong position. Their impatience is their downfall. They wanted the progress but rejected the process.

OPPORTUNITY COMES TO THOSE WHOSE DESIRE AND DECISIONS PLACE THEM IN THE RIGHT POSITION FOR SUCCESS.

iv. Endurance

So now you find yourself well positioned for opportunity, but it's still not happening. You now need to apply endurance and faith.

You inherit or achieve successfully because of these qualities: endurance, faithfulness, persistence and consistency.

Endurance is the refusal to surrender to whatever comes against you, and the refusal to surrender, brings the ensuing reward. Endurance builds stamina. Stamina has you pressing on or continuing, when everyone else is giving up.

Don't look for short cuts or the easy way out. Keep making the right decisions built on the right desires. If you believe you are on the right course in life, continue to apply faithfulness and patience and you will fulfil your goals. "But I've done everything right and I'm not seeing the answer. What should I do?" Keep to your course! Keep your eyes on the bigger picture. Be tenacious and hold onto your dreams.

v. Initiative

The fifth step to living a life of opportunity is initiative. Initiative makes things happen.

In the beginning **God created** the heavens and the earth.[30]

Now that's initiative! We are made in the image of a creative God. Don't fear initiative and entrepreneurialism ... you were born for it! And don't be fearful about money; its a tool to help you accomplish great things when you handle it correctly. Money in itself, is neither good nor evil.

Money takes on the characteristics of those in whose hands it finds itself. For example, if a gambler has money, it is gambling money. In the hands of a drug runner it's drug money. If this same money should find it's way into your hands, it will take on your character. If you have integrity, then money in your hands is also integrous.

Jesus was much more impressed with a man who was entrusted with five talents (a form of currency), invested it and doubled it, than He was with another who was given one talent, hid it and kept it.

"Well done good and faithful servant" He said to the investor who doubled his money. To the one who hid what he had in the ground, Jesus said what he had would be taken away. Hard times were ahead for the unprofitable servant.

In other words, Jesus was encouraging entrepreneurialism. In fact His life championed extraordinary initiative, which subjected Him to conflict and criticism.

We must build into our lives a DESIRE for opportunity. We then commit ourselves to making DECISIONS which line up with our desire. With this combination in place, we are then well POSITIONED for opportunity. ENDURANCE keeps us committed to our course and with INITIATIVE we inherit the promised opportunities of life. This is the process of progress.

Progress toward your own personal life's purpose, must be the goal, but this will not happen coincidentally. You must be committed to giving your life the correct impetus, which enables you to negotiate with power every bend and curve on the highway of life.

You can get a powerful and productive life!

Life is about progress. The process for progress meets the challenges, learns the lessons, takes the time, fights the battles, runs the race and finishes the course. If you want your destiny, accept and enjoy the journey. Be prepared for opportunity and ... GET A LIFE!

TAKE ACTION

1. **Determine** what impetus your life is receiving. **Stop coasting**.

2. Accept the process for progress. **Count the cost** and be tenacious.

3. Decide that you are going to **complete every task** before you, no matter how difficult it is.

4. **Remove** any internal obstacles to progress and **prepare for the long haul**. No quick-fix solutions.

5. Determine not to be bullied into mediocrity by potential-limiting pseudo-knowledge. Commit to being genuinely and extraordinarily effective. **Think about small steps forward**, and encourage yourself through them.

6. Decide today "I am committed to living a life that **points to the solutions**, not the problems."

7. **Position** yourself for opportunity and practise initiative.

EPILOGUE

Wisdom is **a tree of life** to those who take hold of it and **happy are all who retain it.**

PROVERBS 3:18

EPILOGUE

You can know every principle in this book and understand how it works, but without the WISDOM to apply the principles to your life they are useless to you.

> Wisdom is a **TREE of life** to those who take hold of it, and **happy** are all who retain it.[31]

In this proverb, wisdom is compared to a tree.

Imagine a tall gum tree standing on a riverbank; its old weather-beaten trunk twisting high into the sky. Thick green foliage covers the branches. Waters rise during a time of flooding. Tremendous pressure is placed on that tree by the brown swirling current, but it doesn't move. Hurricane winds blast it and force it to lean over. It still won't move because its roots are deep in the ground.

Like that tree, wisdom is our strength, our foundation, our deep root system.

Remember, there may be bends and curves along the way with life's unexpected twists, but the wise come out of the turns moving upwards. They don't spiral downward every time something goes wrong.

Yes, there will be circumstances and events that take us by surprise, but applying wisdom to them will cause us to learn and develop. It moves us onward and upward.

Wisdom Will Promote You

Wisdom promotes you to a better life. It requires a change in the way you think. To live with purpose means enlarging and raising your thought patterns. It will take an elevation of your thinking and a determination not to be conformed into the thought patterns of society. Refuse to be squeezed into the mould of people who aren't pursuing their destiny.

Be TRANSFORMED in your thinking, taking on a whole new MINDSET which in turn will create a new life of abundance and favour. You never have a resolute and improved life if you do not allow wisdom to promote you.

There are many individuals in this world with no ambition, no expectation for a better job or happier home and no desire to progress. Frankly, these people don't believe such things are possible for them. They can only see the negative side of change; the sacrifice, the hard work and the risks.

Wisdom Means Wise Choices

A lack of wisdom or a lack of applied knowledge in daily living, causes people to live at a level well below what is readily available to them. For example, a person may defend their right to smoke, but it is obvious that while smoking is not illegal, it certainly isn't beneficial.

Wisdom means applying commonsense principles to your day-to-day decisions. Building a disciplined way of living on a foundation of expectation and hope. Such wisdom is a "tree of life."

Wisdom Is Available In Generous Supply

Have you ever wondered where we can find enough wisdom to keep us on the right track, maintain happiness, provide longevity, build richness and pleasantness, bring high self-esteem, attract favour and promotion, and cause us to live with discipline and discretion?

The truth is, wisdom is not in short supply.

It is through knowledge that I know when I press a light switch I will enable a light to glow. Through understanding I can comprehend the intricacies of electrical current and therefore why the light works. I require WISDOM to actually DO what I both know and understand.

Too many people know and understand the principles of life and yet do not have the wisdom to apply them to their lives.

Wisdom will increase as you apply it to your life. It will be an invaluable companion on your journey through life. Getting wisdom is the key to unlocking the door to a higher level of life.

> "Knowledge is proud that he has learn'd so much; Wisdom is humble that he knows no more." (*William Cowper 1785*)

Within these pages is the door to the life you

previously only dreamed possible, and applying wisdom is your key to that door.

You CAN make that life a reality. Regardless of your chosen field of endeavour, regardless of your current circumstances, the quality of your life WILL BE TRANSFORMED in direct proportion to your degree of commitment to apply wisdom to these principles.

You can leave mediocrity behind forever and ex-change it for an abundant and fulfilling life, the life you were created for.

From this day forward desire a great future and collide with your destiny. You need to daily decide to fight all negativity and believe only for the very best. You have to guard your mind and your thoughts. Hold on to your dream. Start well and don't slow down ... be there at the finish line. Take hold of every opportunity and seek wisdom to guide you into all that awaits you.

In other words: GET A LIFE! OBTAIN THE LIFE YOU WERE BORN TO ENJOY!

REFERENCES

1. Ecclesiastes 9:4
2. Ecclesiastes 9:11
3. Ecclesiastes 9:11
4. Ecclesiastes 9:12
5. Matthew 12:34
6. Proverbs 13:20
7. Proverbs 18:1
8. Proverbs 27;:6
9. Proverbs 12:25
10. Matthew 7:3
11. Proverbs 22:6
12. 3 John 2
13. Proverbs 16:9
14. Proverbs 4:23
15. Proverbs 20:21
16. Proverbs 23:7
17. Proverbs 19:2
18. Proverbs 1:5, 9:9
19. Proverbs 14:2
20. Proverbs 18:21
21. Proverbs 10:11
22. Proverbs 10:19
23. Proverbs 10:32
24. Proverbs 29:18
25. Proverbs 3:13, 16
26. Psalm 126:5
27. Proverbs 23:7
28. Proverbs 15:19
29. Genesis 1:1
30. Proverbs 3:18
31. Proverbs 4:7

For further information on other books and resource
material by Brian Houston, write to:

Brian Houston Ministries
PO Box 1195, Castle Hill
NSW 1765 AUSTRALIA